A "Bully" First Lady: Edith Kermit Roosevelt

A "Bully" First Lady:
Edith Kermit Roosevelt

Tom Lansford

Nova History Publications, Inc.
Huntington, New York

Senior Editors: Susan Boriotti and Donna Dennis
Coordinating Editor: Tatiana Shohov
Office Manager: Annette Hellinger
Graphics: Wanda Serrano
Book Production: Matthew Kozlowski, Jonathan Rose and Jennifer Vogt
Circulation: Cathy DeGregory, Ave Maria Gonzalez and Raheem Miller
Communications and Acquisitions: Serge P. Shohov

Library of Congress Cataloging-in-Publication Data
Available Upon Request

ISBN 1-59033-086-2.

Copyright © 2001 by Nova History Publications, a division of
Nova Science Publishers, Inc.
227 Main Street, Suite 100
Huntington, New York 11743
Tele. 631-424-NOVA (6682)   Fax 631-425-5933
E Mail: Novascience@earthlink.net

Printed in the United States of America

For Cindy and David

CONTENTS

PREFACE

Edith Roosevelt was one half of one of the most powerful and influential political couples in American history. Edith proved to be a perfect complement to her husband Theodore as her quiet nature and self-assured nature balanced the exuberance and recklessness of her husband. She was mother to the largest family of children ever to live in the White House and is rated as one of the more efficient and competent First Ladies. Yet, she is also a figure that is cloaked in relative obscurity. After Theodore's death, Edith refused offers to write an autobiography and instead continued to work to promote the memory of her husband and his political legacy. Towards the end of her life, Edith slipped into obscurity and was far overshadowed by her relative, Eleanor Roosevelt. In this regard, Edith was able to maintain the privacy that had marked her life even after her death.

Although she did not have the public persona of later First Ladies, Edith was truly the first modern First Lady and she initiated a number of innovations and customs that were adopted by subsequent presidential spouses. She revolutionized the manner in which the White House utilized the press by instituting a variety of strategies to carefully craft the image of herself, her husband and her family. Edith was the first presidential spouse to employ a social secretary and she brought a level of proficiency and management to the White House that had been unseen prior to her husband's election. In 1902, she also oversaw one of the most significant renovations of the White House which separated the official offices of the Executive Mansion to the West Wing while expanding the family's personal space.

Edith's mania for privacy limited the resources that future biographers would be able to access. In addition, her efforts toward this end during her lifetime also curtailed the information that was available to the press and public. As a result, future works on Edith Kermit Carow Roosevelt would be based to a large extent on the impressions of her held by friends and family members. For while Edith was reserved and reticent to expose herself and her private life, the rest of the Roosevelt clan were prolific writers. Theodore and the children wrote numerous works about the family and Edith. In addition, much of their correspondence has been collected in various works (Edith destroyed a large amount of her own letters and correspondence before her death).

This work is an endeavor to provide readers with an overview of both Edith's character and personality and her accomplishments as political wife. As such, it delves into the intricacies of her relationships with Theodore, their children and other members of the Roosevelt family. It traces the degree to which the complexities of these relationships shaped Edith's life and her legacy as the matriarch of the Oyster Bay branch of the Roosevelt clan. Concurrently, the work examines the considerable political contributions Edith made. This includes her roles as soldier's and minor politician's wife to her time as First Lady of both the state of New York and of the United States. As such, the work is both a homage and critical appraisal of a "Bully" First Lady.

ACKNOWLEDGMENTS

Most scholarly endeavors of this sort are not individual accomplishments, but rather the culmination of the work of many. I would like to thank Robert P. Watson, who in addition to being the nation's foremost scholar on first ladies, is a colleague and friend with whom I have worked with on a variety of projects. This work and the others in this series are the result of his inspiration and hard work in developing the program. I would also like to thank my colleagues at New England College, Patrick Hayden, Wayne Lesperance and Jim Walsh, for their intellectual support during the preparation of the manuscript. As always, my thanks go out to Mr. James D. Buffett for assistance in the writing and editing of the work. The staff at the Library of Congress were most helpful and their professionalism is greatly appreciated, as was the assistance of the archivists at the Widener and Houghton Libraries, Harvard University. I am also thankful for the access provided by the staff at the Theodore Roosevelt Birthplace National Historic Site in New York City. Finally, as always, my special thanks go out to Amber for helping me through this work (and for putting-up with me).

INTRODUCTION

Edith Kermit Carow Roosevelt provided an air of dignity, grace and attention to family which served as the perfect counterweight to the intense energy and ambition of her husband, Theodore "Teddy" Roosevelt. She also proved to be an adept household and financial manager throughout her life. As such she was able to maintain a standard of living for her family which initially exceeded the fiscal constraints of public office and Teddy's often exorbitant spending habits. While First Lady, the White House again became the social center of Washington. She was the first First Lady to hire a full-time social secretary. During Teddy's political career, she was also able to preserve the privacy of the family and raise six children as a close-knit family despite the intrusiveness of public life. Edith's role as "balancer" to her husband and her reestablishment of White House social patterns made Edith a natural bridge from the nineteenth to the twentieth century.

WIFE AND MOTHER

Edith Kermit Carow and Theodore Roosevelt were childhood acquaintances. They grew up in the same neighborhood in New York City and had a number of mutual friends. Edith would eventually become Theodore's sister Corrine's best friend. After the death of his first wife, Alice Lee, Theodore married Edith in London in 1886. Roosevelt had one daughter from his first marriage, and he and Edith ultimately had five children from their marriage. Throughout the marriage, Edith often referred to Theodore as sixth of her children.[1] While Theodore often played with the children, engaging in various sports and games, Edith played the role of the responsible adult.

Theodore's exuberance was matched by Edith's calm, reserved manner. This extended to most areas of the marriage. For instance, while Roosevelt often spent beyond the family's means, Edith served as a competent household manager and ensured that the family maintained fiscal solvency. In addition, Roosevelt spent much of his time away from the family, hunting or involved in political campaigns. Edith often found herself left alone to oversee the family and manage the home. This remained true both during Roosevelt's political career and after he retired following his unsuccessful bid for the presidency in 1912.

Edith's reserved manner was partially the result of her nature and partially the result of the circumstances of her marriage. Although Edith and Theodore had a close marriage, she never forgot that she was his second choice for marriage. Theodore's first wife Alice was prettier than Edith and had a much more outgoing nature. Alice died at the age of twenty-three, and Edith was aware that her untimely death meant that she forever remained young and beautiful in Theodore's mind. Roosevelt's actions often exacerbated these feelings. He kept his courtship with Edith quiet and their engagement announcement in the *New York Times* surprised many, including Roosevelt's two sisters, Bamie and Corrine.[2] A sign of Roosevelt's inability to fully deal with his first wife's death was his refusal to call his daughter from his first marriage by her name because it reminded him of Alice Lee. Instead of using "Alice," Roosevelt consistently called her "Baby Lee."

The family home, Sagamore Hill at Oyster Bay, New York, had originally been built for Alice Lee, but following her marriage, Edith quickly placed her stamp on the estate. Through the years, Sagamore Hill became Edith's refuge away from the intricacies and difficulties of public life. She allowed Theodore to choose most of the furnishings, but arranged one room as a personal parlor. The room was simply furnished and Edith's favorite piece of furniture was a writing desk that was inherited from her Aunt Kermit. While they were at Sagamore Hill, Edith would spend her mornings doing correspondence and

---

[1] Betty Boyd Caroli, *First Ladies* (New York: Oxford University Press, 1995), p. 119.

[2] The surprise was so great that the two women forced the paper to retract the announcement since they thought it had to be untrue.

overseeing the family's business. Meanwhile, Theodore used the time to work on his writings. Often the couple used the afternoons to go rowing or hiking.[3]

Edith was the center of the Roosevelt family. Theodore was often absent, initially because of his political career and travels, and later because of his untimely death. As a result, Edith raised the children essentially by herself. The exception to this was Alice or Baby Lee who spent considerable time with her maternal grandparents, the Lees. Edith and Alice never became close and the two had strained relations through the mother's lifetime. The same incredible stock of patience that made her such a good match for Theodore made Edith a remarkable mother. Much of Roosevelt's energy was passed on to the children. They were often rambunctious and tested the bounds of behavior. Through all of their pranks and childhood antics, Edith's patience prevailed and she maintained a degree of composure that was enviable.

When Edith entered the White House as first lady, her children ranged in age from the seventeen-year-old Alice to Quentin who was just three-years-old when his father became president. This disparity in age, while not uncommon in families at the time, presented special problems as Edith had to oversee Alice's stormy passage into adulthood and deal with the usual pranks and demands of toddlers simultaneously. Complicating matters further was Theodore's often childlike behavior. In spite of the differences in age, the family remained close-knit throughout Edith's life. After Theodore's death, Edith traveled extensively, including journeys to Japan and Mexico, but she remained the foundation of the family.

Throughout her husband's political career, Edith helped craft a carefully designed image of the family. Unlike her husband, she was acutely aware of the impact of the family's actions on the press and public. Throughout her time as a political wife, Edith demonstrated an uncanny appreciation of public perceptions and developed a variety of strategies to control the dissemination of information about her family. For example, she often arranged for posed photographs to be taken of the family and then distributed to the press. In this way, she could control the public's impressions about the family.

---

[3] Sylvia Jukes Morris, *Edith Kermit Roosevelt: Portrait of a First Lady* (Coward, McCann & Geoghegan, Inc., 1980), pp. 110-11.

ROLE AS FIRST LADY

Unlike many First Ladies, Edith possessed a high degree of self-confidence and self-assurance. Her years with Theodore and her experience both as First Lady of New York and her brief tenure as the wife of the Vice President, had helped prepare her for the responsibilities and pressures of being First Lady. Edith initially opposed Roosevelt's decision to accept President William McKinley's offer to become Vice-President. She quietly waited for the end of his term of office in 1908 and opposed his effort to run for the presidency in 1912.

As First Lady, Edith had three main priorities. First and foremost, she wanted to ensure the privacy of her family. In order to safeguard the family from the intrusiveness of the press and public, Edith initiated a variety of innovations in the White House. Through the White House renovation of 1902, she separated the president's private residence from the offices and rooms used for official functions. In this manner she was able to isolate the family quarters from what she termed as the "store." She also hired a social secretary not only to help her manage the hectic schedules of office, but also to establish an intermediary between her and both the press and social obligations. Second, Edith sought to restrain Theodore from his excesses. Although, she would not rebuke him in public, Edith did not hesitate to let Theodore know when she felt he had stepped out of line. She often gave him political advice and even monitored his correspondence. Third, and finally, she engaged in a proactive strategy to manage the press. Edith was aware that the public was fascinated with the young family, which contrasted sharply with the more staid McKinleys. With their high spirits and quirks such as the menagerie of animals they brought into the White House, the Roosevelts provoked a large degree of curiosity among the American people. Edith effectively managed the press to a degree unseen by First Ladies.

Noted First Ladies scholar Robert P. Watson identifies seven primary roles of the presidential spouse. Watson categories these roles as

(a) White House historian, decorator, preservationist, archivist, and chief executive officer; (b) the social and ceremonial hostess for the White House and entire nation; (c) the nation's conscience and advocate for causes and social projects; (d) presidential envoy, diplomat, or surrogate; (e) campaigner and promoter of the president and presidential policies and full political and presidential partner; (f) symbol of the American woman; and (g) supportive wife and mother.[4]

In most of these roles, Edith excelled. She oversaw a major renovation of the White House in 1902 and arranged two of the major social events in the nation during the Roosevelt's time in office (the marriage of Alice Lee to Nicolas Longworth and her daughter Ethel's social debut). After several years in which the social center of Washington had moved away from the White House, mainly because of Ida McKinley's health problems, Edith restored the executive mansion as the capital of Washington society. She further exercised a degree of fiscal and staff management that was equaled by few presidential spouses. Her skillful control of the press helped promote both Theodore and the family. Finally, she was certainly was a devoted wife and the backbone of the family. Although she worked with a variety of charities, including the Needlework Guild which provided clothing for the poor, Edith was not a social campaigner on the order of Eleanor Roosevelt or other later first ladies. Nor was Edith a "copresident"[5] who helped her husband achieve political goals through direct political action. Although Theodore often turned to her for political advise, and generally respected her political acumen, Edith preferred to remain out of the limelight and away from the frontlines of politics.

Edith was not the greatest first lady in presidential history. Several polls that ranked the presidential spouses categorized Edith as an "average" first lady. A poll by the Siena Research Institute in 1993 ranked Edith as number 14 among 37 first ladies, while a poll conducted by Robert P. Watson ranked Edith as number 12 (along with Lucretia Rudolph Garfield, Abigail Powers Fillmore, Elizabeth McCardle Johnson and Hillary Rodham Clinton) among 39 first ladies..[6] However, Edith was the perfect partner for Theodore. She both complemented her husband's strengths and concurrently augmented his weaknesses. While she may not have been a great first lady in her own right, Edith provided the base and stability necessary for Theodore's political success.

---

[4] Robert P. Watson, "Incorporating the First Lady into the Classroom," *Social Studies* 89/4 (Jul/Aug 1998), p. 166.

[5] Ibid.

[6] For an overview of these polls and explanations of their methodology, see Robert P. Watson, "Ranking the Presidential Spouses," *Social Science Journal* 36/1 (1999) pp. 117-32.

Edith Roosevelt's life was marked by a devotion to husband and family. After Theodore's death, she remained the center of the Roosevelt clan. She also assumed a more active role in politics, even campaigning against her nephew Franklin in the 1932 presidential election. Besides suffering the loss of her beloved husband "Teedie" in 1919, Quentin Roosevelt died in 1918 while serving as a fighter pilot in World War I. Her other sons survived the First World War, but World War II would bring devastating losses to Edith. Between the wars, Kermit began to drink heavily and he ultimately committed suicide in Alaska in 1943 (although Edith was told that he died of heart failure). Edith's eldest son, Theodore Junior, died of a heart attack at age 56 while commanding American troops during the invasion of Normandy in 1944, during World War II (for his actions Theodore was awarded the Medal of Honor and became the most decorated American soldier of World War II). In spite of her personal tragedies, Edith continued to face life with self-confidence and with the efficiency for which she was known. She worked to preserve and protect her husband's memory and to sustain the grandeur of the Roosevelt family name. Edith continued to manage the family's estate with her usual meticulousness. She even preplanned her own funeral in great detail.

An intensely private person, Edith always preferred to remain out of the spotlight and use her talents to promote husband and family. This work is an effort to cast light on a life that was often overshadowed by those around Edith. It is further an analysis of the traits and characteristics of a model first lady whose greatness centered around her ability to balance her husband. In doing so, Edith was one-half of one of the most successful political couples in American history. Yet Edith's accomplishments also ranged beyond those of spouse. As First Lady she instituted a variety of innovations which helped chang the nature of the role of future first ladies. As such, she truly was the "first" modern First Lady of the twentieth century.

Chapter 1

"Edie" and "Teedie", The Early Years

E dith Kermit Carow was born on August 6, 1861 to a family line that could trace its American ancestry back to 1638. Among Edith's more prominent ancestors was the noted Puritan clergyman Jonathan Edwards (1703-1758) who was active during the early religious revival known as the Great Awakening. Her parents were Charles Carow and Gertrude Tyler Carow. Charles was the descendent of French Huguenots who had arrived in New York in 1685, and Gertrude was descended from Job Tyler, an early English immigrant. Edith was born in Norwich Connecticut, but in March of 1864, the family moved to a brownstone in Union Square in New York City.

Edith grew-up as a neighbor of the Roosevelt clan. Her parents were friends of the Roosevelts. Edith and Theodore's sister Corrine were born only two months apart and grew-up as close friends. Edith and Corrine or "Conie" would remain fast friends until her marriage to Theodore created tensions between the two. Conie often visited Edith and eventually her two brothers also began spending time at the Carow home. Edith met Theodore when she was four and he was seven. The young girl often traveled to the Roosevelt summer house at Oyster Bay, Long Island and spent time with the family. Despite their age difference, the two became friends and were known to each other as "Edie" and "Teedie." During the summers at Oyster Bay, Edith often accompanied Theodore as he rowed, and at one point, the young Roosevelt named his rowboat after her.[1]

---

[1] H.W. Brands, *TR: The Last Romantic* (New York: Basic Books, 1997), p. 52.

Edith was blonde-haired and had bright blue eyes. As a child, Edith was quiet and reserved. Yet she was also intelligent and clever. As she grew, the young girl developed a love of reading and an insatiable appetite for books. Much of her time was spent reading. While she engaged in the range of activities that other children did, playing games and hiking in the woods, her happiest times were reading. Still Edith was always very aware of her appearance and dressed immaculately. She would eventually be known by many of her friends as "Spotless Edie."[2] During her youth, Edith had several close friends, but she also preferred her solitude and spent countless hours alone reading. Her interest in literature would ultimately serve as one of the bond between her and Theodore.

She had one sibling, a sister named Emily who was born on April 18, 1865. Charles and Gertrude also had a son who died in 1860 when he was only six-months-old. Her early childhood was comfortable and she and her sister were raised principally by an Irish nanny, Mary Ledwith. However, as she grew-up, her family began to experience some troubles. Both parents eventually suffered from a variety of ailments, some real and some imagined. Her father began to drink heavily and this significantly affected his health. He eventually became an alcoholic. Gertrude was also afflicted by a number of ailments such as arthritis and gout. Most importantly, in the aftermath of the Civil War, the Carow family began to have financial troubles. Charles's drinking and postwar inflation severely damaged finances of the Kermit & Carow shipping company.

The Roosevelts were aware of the family's money problems, and at one point Theodore's mother Mittie arranged for the Carow girls to have kindergarten classes with her children in order to save the Carows this additional expense.[3] This shared experience had the affect of bringing Edie and Teedie even closer together. The two studied together and Edie often read aloud to Teedie. They particularly enjoyed works which were romantic and presented the old-fashioned virtues of men and women.[4]

Financial problems for the Carow family reached dramatic levels when Edith was six. The family was forced to leave their home and for some time survived by living with relatives. In 1867, the family moved in with an aunt,

---

[2]Theodore Roosevelt, Jr. *All in the Family* (New York: Putnam, 1929), p. 58.

[3] Morris, p. 16.

[4] Theodore Roosevelt, *Autobiography* (New York: Macmillan, 1913), p. 17.

Ann Eliza Kermit. However, the aunt's house was even closer to the Roosevelt mansion and Edith began to spend even more time with the inner circle of Roosevelt children and their closest friends. During the summers, the Carows would travel to Red Bank, New Jersey, where Gertrude's father, Daniel, had a summer home.

By the late 1860s, Charles Carow's drinking had reached crisis proportions and by this point, the man had become a full alcoholic. In addition to problems with the family shipping company, the economic depressions of 1869 and 1873 drastically reduced the family's wealth. For the remainder of his life, Charles made sporadic efforts to find new employment. However, he had little success and each successive failure reinforced his self-doubts and increased his health problems.

THE INNER CIRCLE

In her youth, Edith spent considerable time with the Roosevelts. In New York City, Edith was often at the Roosevelts, not just for kindergarten, but also for play. In addition, during the summers, she stayed with the family at their estate on Long Island. Although Edith remained close to her mother, Mittie Roosevelt also served as something of a surrogate mother. The accomplished and strong-willed Mittie presented a very different figure than the fragile Gertrude. Besides being matriarch of the Roosevelt clan, Mittie was involved in a variety of activities and the children delighted in her stories about growing-up in the antebellum South. Much of Edith's self-composure and her self-assurance can be traced to Mittie's influence. Theodore Roosevelt Senior, Teedie's father, also had a significant impact on Edith's life, although his influence was mainly concentrated in educational matters. He often lectured to the children in the Roosevelt Kindergarten about his experiences and arranged various trips for the children to museums and natural areas. He even wrote plays for the class to perform. The Roosevelt home provided an atmosphere where Edith's intellect could be nurtured and exposed her to a wider range of culture.

Just as Mittie Roosevelt had a tremendous influence on Edith, Mittie's sister, Anna Bulloch Gracie, also played a major role in shaping the girl's future. Anna or "Annie" served as the children's kindergarten instructor. Between Mittie and Annie, Edith was in capable hands. Besides teaching

Edith the basics of reading, writing and arithmetic, Annie also taught Edith needlework. In time, the young girl became extremely proficient at sewing and various styles of needlework. This past time became a favorite form of diversion for Edith and it remained an enjoyable type of recreation throughout her life.

As a child, Edith's closest friends were her sister Ellie, and Conie and Teedie Roosevelt. These relationships which were formed in her youth, remained the cornerstone of Edith's adult connections. The relationship between Conie and Edie was often uneven. As girls, the two were very close and ultimately became best friends. As time went by, however, tensions frequently arose between the two. In many ways the two girls were polar opposites. Corrine was outgoing and extroverted while Edith often kept to herself and was introverted. In addition, Conie was the more playful of the two, while Edie usually carried herself with a seriousness that belied her young age. They were bound together by a passion for literature and poetry and by their fondness for Conie's brother. However, this attraction for Theodore would often lead to jealously between the two, especially later in life.

Edith's relationship with Theodore was also highly complicated. From their earliest meeting the two had an affinity for each other which only grew through the years. Like Conie, Theodore enjoyed Edith's intellectual company. He especially liked to have her read to him, and he relished discussing literature with her. During the summers that she spent at Oyster Bay, Edith often went rowing or on hikes with Theodore. Later, when the Roosevelt family traveled, the two engaged in a lively and lengthy correspondence. Despite the fact that she was younger than he, Theodore found his "Edie" to be more mature than many of his acquaintances.

On the other hand, Edith did not share Theodore's enthusiasm for physical activity. While many of the children engaged in a variety of sports and athletic endeavors, Edith favored her reading. Although she did not dislike pets, and was very fond of several during her life, Edith did not share Teedie's passion for animals. In addition, the two had very different temperaments. Theodore relished company while Edith preferred her solitude or the companionship of a few friends. As the two children grew into adolescence their interest in each other evolved differently. Over time, Edith's fondness for Theodore developed into a love that would eventually dominate her life. Theodore counted Edith as one of his closest friends, but his love for her would come later in life.

In 1869, the Roosevelts embarked upon a tour of Europe. The extended travel would ultimately last a year and mark the first of several such trips. While his brother and sisters looked forward to the journey, Theodore was heartbroken to leave Edith. He wrote in his diary that it was ". . . hard parting from our friend."[5] While Theodore was gone, he and Edith carried-on a lively correspondence, especially for two children their age (Edith was eight and Theodore was eleven). Many of the letters expressed how much Teedie missed Edie. At one point on the trip, Theodore record in his diary that a picture of Edie ". . . stirred up in me homesickness and longings for the past which will come again never, alack never."[6]

ADOLESCENCE

While the Roosevelts were in Europe, the classes that Edith had been attending were discontinued. The Carow family discussed sending Edith to another school, but monetary considerations prevented full-time enrollment. Instead the young girl was enrolled at a school that taught dance and deportment. Edith became a polished dancer. Upon their return in 1870, the Roosevelt children also joined the school. To the chagrin of Theodore's sisters, Edith was one of the most popular dance partners among the boys at the school. In the end, Edith saved most of her dances for Theodore.[7]

In 1871, the Roosevelts decided to move and they were soon followed by the Carows. Gertrude and the two sisters traveled to Pennsylvania while Charles tried to find the family a house. Concurrently, her parents had decided to send Edith to school. Charles eventually found a home on West Forty-Fourth Street. In the fall, Edith was enrolled at a private school operated by Louise Comstock. Miss Comstock's School, as it was known, was an exclusive and expensive preparatory school for young ladies. Edith would attend with a family friend, Fanny Smith.

While at the school, Edith's character became set. Her studious nature was reinforced and she found her intellectual horizon expanded as she was introduced to an ever-increasing variety of both popular and classical

---

[5] Theodore Roosevelt, *Diaries of Boyhood and Youth* (New York: Charles Scribner's Sons, 1928), p. 13.

[6] Ibid., p. 103.

[7] Morris, p. 27.

literature. In keeping with her inclination Edith did well in the arts and humanities, however she had little aptitude for the sciences or languages. She did poorly in German, but eventually became fluent in both written and spoken French. Edith enjoyed the works of William Shakespeare and many of the classic authors and poets of English literature. She often carried works by the Bard with her, even later in life, so that when opportunities presented themselves she could read. Edith's obsession with literature became so pronounced that it interfered with her other studies. Eventually the young woman was forced to establish a personal rule for herself not to read novels or poems that were not related to her studies while she was in school.[8]

In addition to her formal studies, the Comstock School also provided education in a variety of other areas. For instance, while at the school Edith developed the deep moral convictions and religiosity that would mark her character for the rest of her life. The headmistress, Louise Comstock, based most of her lessons on religious themes. Edith seems to have taken these themes to heart. By the time she finished school, the young woman was a devout Christian with a strong sense of morality.

The Comstock School also exposed Edith the finest areas of New York Society. She attended symphonies and other musical performances. Edith also regularly visited museums and other live performances, including plays. Edith and her friend Fanny, often went together to see Shakespearian plays around the city. Edith was tutored on a variety of writing techniques and ultimately developed her own style. This style was the logical result of someone who sought to improve her speed in writing because of the large amount of correspondence she wrote and the significant amount of notes she took. Throughout her time at the school, Edith regularly penned letters to Theodore, especially on those occasions when the Roosevelt family were on one of their tours, such as the 1872-73 journey which took them to the Mediterranean and Europe.

This tour had lasted just over a year and upon the return of the Roosevelts, Edith seems to have begun her initial infatuation with Theodore. Concurrently, however, sixteen-year-old Theodore began to drift away from twelve-year-old Edie. He became more absorbed with his studies and his preparations for entry into Harvard. The two still saw each other at social

---

[8] Edith Roosevelt to Kermit Roosevelt, Letter, April 21 1907, Kermit Roosevelt Papers, Library of Congress, Washington, D.C.

functions, but their main periods where they spent time together was during the summers when Edith continued her habit of traveling to Oyster Bay.

While in Europe, Corrine became a member of a literary club. When she returned to the United States she started her own among her circle of friends. The club was initially known as the "Paradise of Ravenous Eaters" or P.O.R.E., although the words were later changed to "Party of Renowned Eligibles." The club lasted three years and included Corrine, Edie, Fanny Smith and nine others. The club served as an outlet for its members to share their poetry and narrative writings. Edith was appointed the secretary and during the meetings of the club, she made copies of stories and poems that members produced. During the three-year period that P.O.R.E. existed, Edith's writings matured and she became quite adept at dealing with complicated themes.

From 1872 to 1875, Edith divided her summers between her Grandfather's estate in New Jersey and the Roosevelt summer house at Oyster Bay. Although Edith enjoyed spending time in New Jersey, the area was not as fashionable as Oyster Bay. In addition, her few friends were in Long Island with the Roosevelts. In July of 1874, Theodore came down to New Jersey and spent the last week with Edith. However, the young man spent much of his time exploring the flora and fauna of the area.

When Edith visited Tranquility, the name of the Roosevelt estate at Oyster Bay, she found that the children were given free range of the property. Days were usually spent swimming, hiking and rowing. It was during this period that Theodore christened his rowboat in her honor. The two often went for long boat rides in the afternoon, although Theodore also took other girls, including Fanny Smith, with him on these excursions. The youths also went riding and spent countless hours discussing and debating literature. In many ways, Tranquility was an apt description for both the setting and the experiences during those summer months. In later times, Edith would look back at her time at the Roosevelt estate as one of the happiest periods of her life.

In spite of overall good times, there were dark clouds on the horizon for Edith. Her family's financial problems continued to way heavily on Edith and her future prospects. There were also growing strains between Edith and both Theodore and Corrine. Theodore was preparing to go to Harvard and while he genuinely enjoyed his Edie's company, a host of other concerns occupied his attention. For instance, in preparation for Harvard, Roosevelt studied diligently. His interests in science and forensics led him to go hunting for the purpose of securing specimens to examine. He often brought multiple animal carcasses back to the house for analysis and study. Edith had little desire to participate in Theodore's studies of this nature. Still, while many girls found Theodore's habits and his personality strange, Edith continued her infatuation. She found Teedie fascinating. The young woman particularly liked what she termed his "character" and "enthusiasms." More significantly, Theodore shared Edith's high sense of morality. In this regard the two were closely matched in personality, even though their temperaments were markedly different.

Tensions between Edith and Corrine grew during this period. The personality differences between the two girls were exacerbated by adolescence. By their mid-teens the love-hate relationship of the two evolved into the pattern that would continue throughout the lives of both women. While the two were very fond of each other, several areas would tend to strains and even outright periods of hostility. Edith had grown into a lovely young women. She was tall and had golden hair and pleasant features. Corrine was intimidated by Edith's looks. In addition, Edith's serious nature could often be misinterpreted. Her aloofness was sometimes mistaken for scorn, even by her close friends. Corrine also seems to have been threatened by Edith's literary talents and her developed sense of scholarship. Conversely, Edith envied Corrine's openness and ease in social settings.[9] The different social standings of the two must have also affected Edith. The Carows were a once-prominent family in decline, while the Roosevelts continued to gain in ascendency and fame. This was also true of the financial status of both families. The conspicuous wealth of the Roosevelts must have reminded Edith of her family's financial problems. The Roosevelts were exceeding generous with their fortune and often presented friends and associates with gifts and even monetary support–including allowing Edith to attend their private kindergarten sessions.

The main area of contention between Edith and Corrine centered around their relationship with Theodore. Throughout the remainder of their lives there would be a subtle, and at times not so subtle, competition for Theodore's attention and affection. During his teenage years, Theodore was close with both of his sisters. After the death of Theodore Roosevelt, Senior, in 1878,

---

[9] Morris, pp. 49-50.

Bamie stepped in and helped serve as a surrogate parent, especially as Mittie declined. Furthermore, after the death of his first wife, Bamie essentially raised Theodore's daughter Alice. Throughout his political career, Theodore often turned to his sisters for advice and as sounding boards for ideas. The attentions that Theodore presented to Edith irked both sisters, but affected Corrine more than Bamie. Corrine jealously existed at two levels. On the one hand, she resented Theodore's attentions toward Edith since it intruded on her relationship with her brother. On the other hand, she resented Theodore for intruding on her relationship with Edith. Meanwhile, Edith equally resented Theodore's closeness with his sisters. In their youth, the natural affinity of the siblings represented a bond that Edith knew she would never equal. As they grew older, Theodore's inclination to turn to his sisters for political counsel seemed to reinforce Edith's exclusion from the most intimate levels of the family circle.

Chapter 2

SEPARATION AND RETURN

As Theodore prepared to leave for Harvard, Edith realized that his interest in her has fading. His considerable enthusiasm was directed to this new adventure he was about to embark on. More significantly, he spent considerably more time with his sisters than Edith as he made his preparations. For instance, Bamie chose her brother's room. She then helped Theodore decorate and prepare his room. Theodore wrote his mother on the impact of Bamie's decorating that "I do not know what to admire most the curtains, the paper or the carpet. What I would have done without Bamie . . ."[1] In the fall of 1876, Theodore began his collegiate experience.

Edith had little contact with Theodore until Christmas when she attended several parties along with the Roosevelt circle of friends. Edith and Theodore danced and spent time renewing their friendship. Theodore's sibling's invited Edith to visit Harvard with them in May of 1876. The group spent three days at the university. Edith later recalled that she had a wonderful time and met several of Theodore's friends. Following her return to New York, she penned a thank-you in which she stated that "I enjoyed to the utmost every minute of my stay," meanwhile Theodore told Corrine "I don't think I ever saw Edith looking prettier."[2] This visit was followed by Edith's usual summer trip to Oyster Bay. She spent two weeks with the Roosevelts. The group of friends engaged in their usual antics and spent time involved in both athletic

---

[1] Theodore Roosevelt, *Letters*, 1, Elting E. Morison and John Blum, eds. (Cambridge: Harvard University, 1954), p. 16.

[2] Brands, p.70.

endeavors such as rowing and hiking and more intellectual pursuits including debating literature and reading poetry.

During that summer, Theodore was not immune to the charms of other young women. While he clearly liked Edith, it is uncertain that he had the same depth of romantic feelings toward her that she had for him. There was also the age difference. At age nineteen, Roosevelt viewed himself as a mature college man, while Edith at fifteen remained an adolescent in his eyes. After Edith left, Roosevelt made arrangements to call upon a "Miss Boden," but little came of the flirtation.[3]

Other events further widened the distance between Edith and Theodore. Theodore's father fell ill during the fall of 1877. During his Christmas vacation, the younger Roosevelt made the social rounds with his friends, including Edith, but his concern over his father's health deeply troubled him. The elder Roosevelt had bowel cancer, and although his health declined rapidly, he endeavored to hide the true extent of his illness from his family. He died on February 11, 1878. His father's death deeply affected Roosevelt. In the wake of the funeral, he wrote his friend Henry Minot that "these last few days seem like a hideous dream. Father had always been so much with me that is seems as if part of my life had been taken away."[4] Shortly after the funeral, Roosevelt ceased using his nickname and insisted on being called "Theodore."

The Roosevelt sisters remained at their father's side during his illness. Although the two served as each other's main support during the crisis, Corrine also relied upon Edith. The young woman served as an outside party in which Corrine could discuss her father's condition. The tragedy was demonstrative of the relationship between Edith and Corrine. Despite their capacity to quarrel, the two came together in times of crisis.

During the summer of 1878, Roosevelt returned to Oyster Bay. He sent Edith a gift on her birthday on August 6, and waited impatiently for her annual visit. Once Edith arrived at the Roosevelt estate, she found that Theodore wanted to spend most of his time with her. The couple went rowing and sailing. Unlike the visits of the past few years, Edith and Theodore appeared to return to their childhood closeness. The brief period seemed a repeat of summers past. However, events soon took a dramatic turn.

---

[3] Corrine Roosevelt Robinson, *My Brother Theodore Roosevelt*, 1926, pp. 94-95.

[4] Theodore Roosevelt to Henry Minot, February 20, 1878, in Morrison.

On August 20, the two got into a tremendous argument that tore them apart for several years. The exact cause of the disagreement is subject to considerable debate. Initially, neither of the two discussed the matter with their friends and confidants. In fact, Theodore never spoke of it to any length. His only recorded comment on the episode is contained in a letter written to sister Bamie in which he refers to a "break" in their relationship as a result of their "tempers."[5] Surprisingly, even Roosevelt's meticulous diaries are silent on the subject. In the days after the break, he engaged a variety of vigorous physical activities including hunting and riding in an obvious effort to deal with the incident. Within a few days, however, Theodore had returned to his old self and was busily engaged in his favorite activities. When he returned to Harvard, Roosevelt threw himself into his studies and a variety of social engagements.

Edith was also initially silent on the argument. She left on August 30, and there was little discussion of the event with her parents or other members of the family, including her sister. Nor did Edith discuss the matter with Corrine. However, later in life she seems to have either intentionally or tacitly allowed the notion to surface that Theodore had proposed and she had rejected him. Members of the Carow family reported that Theodore had proposed on more than one occasion. On the other hand, there are no records of such proposals in Theodore's diaries. Corrine recounted that her father had forbidden any discussion of such a match before his death.[6] Edith may have allowed the story to circulate in order to protect her feelings. Soon after Theodore returned to Harvard he met the woman who would eventually become his first wife.

INTERREGNUM

In his junior year at Harvard, Roosevelt's social opportunities expanded greatly. He joined a variety of clubs and seemed to grow dramatically in confidence and self-assurance. On October 18, he met Alice Hathaway Lee. Roosevelt instantly fell in love with her. By Christmas, he was determined to marry her. Nonetheless, Roosevelt continued to correspond with Edith and

---

[5] Theodore Roosevelt to Anna Roosevelt Cowles, September 20, 1886; Theodore Roosevelt Birthplace National Historic Site, New York City.

[6] Charleton Putnam, *Theodore Roosevelt: The Formative Years, 1858-1886* (Charles Scribner's Sons, 1958), p. 170.

often asked about her in his letters to his sisters. They also continued to meet on occasion. However, it became clear that there was a growing gulf between the two. When Roosevelt invited his family to Harvard in May, Edith was excluded. Although she did not know it at the time, the purpose of this trip was to introduce Alice to Roosevelt's mother and sisters.

Meanwhile, life continued for Edith. She continued her studies and her literary pursuits. In April of 1879, she won a literary prize for an entry in a competition sponsored by the journal *World*. She also graduated from Miss Comstock's school that summer. Still, Edith was in the midst of a difficult period in her life. Her estrangement from Roosevelt weighed heavily upon her. It was clear that the episode over the summer had deeply impacted their relationship. Although she did not know it, Roosevelt's growing relationship with Alice further eroded their closeness. Edith suffered emotional loss on other fronts as well. On June 30, 1879, Edith's Aunt Ann Kermit died. Edith had been close with her aunt and her death, coming in the midst of Edith's estrangement from Theodore, was doubly hard on the young seventeen-year-old woman. Aunt Ann's writing desk was left to Edith–who greatly treasured the item. She kept the desk throughout her life and used it for her writing and correspondence.

The Carow family moved again during this period. They acquired a larger townhouse, but even the new home did little to cheer Edith. Her main source of comfort during this period continued to be literature. She read constantly and with a voracious appetite for works of all types, including classics as well as new releases. There was also a brief period when Edith thought she might be able to rekindle Theodore's interest. Unbeknownst to her, Theodore had proposed to Alice sometime in May. Alice did not giver her consent, but she did not reject him entirely. Although he continued to ardently pursue Alice, Theodore also appeared to be considering other options or at least trying to preserve his options in case Alice ultimately said "no." He sent Edith a recently released long poem by Owen Meredith for her birthday. In November, he paid a visit to Edith in New York. To all accounts, the two had an enjoyable reunion which was dominated by discussions of the current state of literature. When he returned home, he recorded in his diary that Edith was the "best-read girl I know."[7]

---

[7] Theodore Roosevelt, unpublished diary, entry November 16, 1879, Theodore Roosevelt Papers, Library of Congress, Washington, D.C.

During his Christmas break from Harvard, Roosevelt went to Edith's house and the two had lunch on the day after Christmas. Roosevelt may have been vacillating between the two women. They were the same age and both were attractive, though in different ways. Alice was taller with gray eyes. Her personality closely resembled that of Theodore's sister Corrine. Alice was extroverted and witty. She was socially polished and often the center of attention at social functions. However, she lacked Edith's literary knowledge and her intelligence. But she also lacked Edith's aloofness.

In many ways, Alice also reminded Theodore of his mother. As with Mittie, Alice would eventually center her life around Theodore. She also personified the traditional notion of American femininity and had a childlike quality that she never outgrew.[8] Alice lacked Edith's self-assurance and in contrast with Theodore's childhood friend, Alice was someone who constantly craved Theodore's attention. After they were married, she would eventually define her life by that of her husband.

Edith and Alice met for the first time during Theodore's Christmas vacation. Alice came down to New York to visit Theodore and the two women met just after Christmas. The two realized their rivalry immediately. The meeting may have been the impetus for Alice's acceptance of Theodore's proposal. On January 25, 1880, Alice formally agreed to marry Theodore. After announcing the news to his family, Theodore told Edith, before any formal public announcement.

Edith was heartbroken. She had always imagined that she would marry Theodore. Since childhood, the two had been constant companions and Edith could not conceive of marrying anyone else. Theodore had always been the "man" or at least the main male in her life. As was her nature, however, she hid her disappointment well from most. Only her family and closest friends knew the true depth of her disappointment. As usual, Edith turned to books for solace and comfort. During the period leading up to Theodore's wedding, she continued to attend social functions with Corrine and her other friends, but she certainly had lost much of her zest and appeared even more withdrawn and aloof than before.

Through her ordeal, Edith remained the good friend. Just prior to his wedding, Edith held a dinner party for him on October 13, 1880. She

---

[8] Henry F. Pringle, *Theodore Roosevelt: A Biography* (New York: Harcourt, Brace & World, 1956), p. 31.

congratulated him and presided over the gathering with grace and dignity. Few of the guests were aware of any tension between the two. Edith went to Boston on October 25, and shared a room with Fanny Smith. The two girls spent some time exploring Boston and attended the wedding together. Fanny later recounted that they enjoyed themselves immensely.[9] Any hint of remorse on the part of Edith was well hidden during the ceremony and the reception that followed.

Through her marriage, Alice became part of the Roosevelt circle. The Roosevelt sisters and all of the family friends welcomed Alice–with one notable exception. Edith remained unusually withdrawn and aloof when in Alice's company. She was even more reserved than normal. Nonetheless, the two often found themselves in each other's company. Edith and Corrine remained best friends so that when Edith accompanied Corrine to social events connected with the Roosevelts, she often encountered Alice. However, during this period, Edith tended to socialize even less than previously. She began to purposely avoid many of the minor social functions. Instead of making the rounds of the parties and balls, Edith concentrated on reading and literature. Nevertheless, she faithfully attended her major obligations as her social status required.

In December of 1880, Corrine had her debut. Edith attended the event along with other members of the Roosevelt inner circle, including Bamie, Fanny Smith and Theodore and Alice. The episode was especially trying for Edith. Her father's fortune and business prospects continued to decline. This constrained the family's ability to meet their social obligations. Edith would not have a social debut as most of her friends did. As a result, Corrine's debut emphasized the growing social gap between the two families. By the time she reached twenty, Edith had few social prospects, and more significantly for a young women during this period, she had no prospects for marriage.

The Carow's financial problems led to some speculation that Edith might marry for money in order to help the family. An arranged marriage of this sort was certainly not uncommon during the late 1800s. The Carow family name still carried some prestige and would have offered someone from the rising business class an opportunity to enter the more elite levels of New York society. There was apparently some discussion of Edith and an arranged marriage, but the young woman could not bring herself to actually go initiate

---

[9] Frances Parsons, *Perchance Some Day* (Private Publication, 1951), p. 43.

such an arrangement. Instead, she maintained that "someday, somehow, she would marry Theodore Roosevelt."[10]

Edith's growing isolation was compounded during the spring and summer of 1880, when Corrine began seeing Douglas Robinson. Edith saw even less of her closest friend as the months went by. The courtship was uneven and Corrine seemed unable to make-up her mind as to whether or not Robinson was the love of her life. However, she had not had many male suitors and was reaching the age when many might consider her a spinster. These factors led her to accept Robinson's marriage proposal in the hopes that over time she would grow to love the man. In February of 1881, came Corrine and Robinson's wedding announcement. The news caused a deep conflict within Edith. She was happy to see her friend engaged, but she was secretly resentful about the engagement. This was true even though she was aware that Corrine was not deeply in love with her fiancee. Edith realized that Corrine's impending marriage would even further isolate her.

Corrine and Robinson were married on April 29, 1882. Edith served as one of her eight bridesmaids, but the ceremony was heart-wrenching. Edith later recounted her feelings about the wedding to Corrine in a letter written a few days after the wedding: "if we live to be ninety years old we can never be two girls together again."[11] Matters were made worse for Edith because Robinson had a second home in New Jersey and he and Corrine spent much of their time there.

Edith did continue to see Theodore on occasion. While the newlywed was immensely happy with his wife and married life in general, he still enjoyed Edith's intellectual company. For her part, Edith relished any opportunity to be with Theodore. Prior to the Roosevelt's departure for a four-month trip to Europe during the summer of 1881, Edith and Theodore spent several afternoons together discussing literature and contemporary events. When Roosevelt returned, he announced that he intended to seek the Republican nomination for the state assembly. Although he was only twenty-three years old, Roosevelt gained the nomination and was subsequently elected. Following the election, Edith threw Roosevelt a celebration party. As was so often the case for Edith during this period, the party was a bittersweet

---

[10] Quoted in Morris, p. 67; Edith's prospects and her growing alienation from the Roosevelts are also described in the passage.

[11] Edith Kermit Roosevelt to Corrine Roosevelt Robinson, May 1, 1882, Theodore Roosevelt Collection, Widener and Houghton Libraries, Harvard University, Cambridge, Massachusetts.

occasion. She was proud of Roosevelt's success, but his election meant that he and Alice would have to move to Albany for at least part of the year. This would deprive Edith of her tenuous contacts with Theodore. With her closest friends gone, Edith spent more and more time with Roosevelt's aunt, Annie Gracie (Edith's former kindergarten teacher). The two women often went to social events together. That Edith was seen mainly with an elderly female companion only seemed to confirm for most the impression that she was becoming a spinster.

Edith found that she had less and less contact with both Corrine, her closest friend, and Theodore, who was the love of her life. In addition, on November 30, 1882, Edith's grandfather, Daniel Tyler, died. Edith had been close to her grandfather. Since she was a child, Edith had spent part of every summer at his house in New Jersey. Tyler's death had one positive benefit for Edith. The former Civil War general left $47,000 to Edith's mother. Tyler arranged for the money to be placed in a trust fund with $5,000 annual installments paid out to the family. While the sum was not enough to restore the family's economic stability, it significantly ameliorated their immediate financial distress.

Soon after the death of her grandfather, Edith found that her father was growing increasingly ill. By the winter of 1883, alcoholism had severely weakened Charles Carow and he became confined to his bed. Edith, her mother and sister remained at his bedside as he grew progressively worse. On March 17, 1883, Carow died. Corrine was pregnant at the time of the funeral and did not attend, but neither did Theodore. Edith's companion Annie Gracie did attend as did Alice Lee Roosevelt.

In the summer of 1883, it was announced that Alice was pregnant. The pregnancy was a difficult one. After giving birth to a daughter, Alice Lee, on February 12, 1884, Alice's health rapidly declined. Alice was suffering from kidney failure. Meanwhile, Roosevelt's mother Mittie had contracted typhoid. Roosevelt had been in New York when Alice was born, but he hurried home immediately after he received a telegram urging his return. For sixteen hours, Theodore and his brother and sisters were at the bedside of one of the two dying women. In the morning of February 14, Mittie died. Later that afternoon, Alice passed also. The ordeal was indescribably traumatic for Roosevelt. He had lost the two principal female figures in his life. He was never able to talk about the episode to anyone, including Edith and other members of his family. The diary entry of February 14 has a large black X and the single phrase: "The life has gone out of my life."[12]

Following the deaths of both his mother and sister, Roosevelt went into a period of emotional emptiness. He fully believed that he would never love again. Most significantly, Roosevelt was unable to emotionally bond with his daughter who seemed only to remind him of his departed wife. The young politician tried to numb his grief through his work and he made a renewed commitment to the growing reform movement within the Republican Party.

RENEWAL

Following the funeral, Roosevelt turned to his sister Bamie to care for his newborn. While Bamie raised little Alice, Roosevelt concentrated on his political career. In addition, to his duties as a state assemblyman, Roosevelt served as a delegate from the state of New York at the Republican National Convention of 1884. The experience marked Roosevelt's first real encounter with politics at the national level. Some figures impressed the young assemblyman, though the majority "included many scoundrels."[13] While at the convention, he met and became friends with Massachusetts Senator Henry Cabot Lodge. The two reformist Republicans would remain political allies for most of their careers. They supported the reform candidate, George F. Edmunds, but the nomination went to longtime party stalwart James G. Blaine. Blaine was defeated by Democrat Grover Cleveland in the general election. Roosevelt blamed the defeat on the corruption and cronyism of the leadership of the Republican Party. The experience helped confirm Roosevelt's reformist ideology.

Despite his effort to absorb himself in work, Roosevelt found it difficult to overcome his recent losses. He decided to spend time in the West. Roosevelt declined to seek reelection to the New York State Assembly and instead traveled to the Dakota territory. He spent much of the time hunting and traveling in Wyoming and Montana. Bamie was left to care for his daughter and he seems to have given little thought to impact of his extended absence on his sister or daughter.

---

[12] Brands, p. 162.

[13] Theodore Roosevelt to Anna "Bamie" Roosevelt, June 8, 1884; Morrison.

For Roosevelt, his daughter Alice seemed to remind him of his deceased wife whose death he had never really dealt-with emotionally. Throughout his life, Roosevelt never talked with Alice about her mother. Rather than call his daughter by her name, he consistently referred to her as "Baby Lee." Roosevelt also made a consistent effort to avoid meeting with or talking to his former wife's family. As she grew-up, Alice felt alienated from her father. Relations between the parents and daughter remained strained and Alice was the exception to the otherwise very close relations in the family.

During this period, Edith and Theodore did not see each other at the young man's insistence. For really the first time in their lives, there was no correspondence between the two. In addition, Theodore pointedly asked his sisters not to invite Edith to any of the functions that he attended in the aftermath of the wedding and before his lengthy trip to the Dakotas. The reasons behind Roosevelt's avoidance of Edith were probably varied, but the usually meticulous diaries that he kept are silent on the subject. Edith continued to spend time with his sisters, and ironically saw more of his daughter in the early part of her life than he did, but she respected his wishes and consciously avoided the recent widower. For instance, in June of 1885, Edith resumed her habit of spending summers at Oyster Bay and spent a month at the home of Annie Gracie. Annie's summer house was close by the mansion that Theodore had begun construction of as a home for he and his family. During the visit, Edith spent considerable time with Bamie and even toured the home, known as Leeholm. Just before Roosevelt returned to Leeholm, Edith left to spend time at Corrine's estate in New Jersey. Although Theodore spent the remainder of the summer at Leeholm, where he received numerous visitors and friends, Edith kept her distance. For nineteen months the two managed to avoid each other, even though they had the same friends and traveled in the same circles.

They met by accident in September of 1885. Edith was leaving Bamie's house when she literally ran into Theodore (although there is no direct evidence, in his biography of Roosevelt Edmund Morris suggests the possibility that Bamie secretly arrange the meeting).[14] This experience rekindled the range of feelings between the two. The two began to see each other in private and then at social gatherings. Their mutual interest in each

---

[14] Edmund Morris, *The Rise of Theodore Roosevelt* (New York: Coward, McCann & Geoghegan, 1979), p. 313.

other grew quickly. For Edith, it seemed as if her long awaited desire to marry Theodore was close to being realized. Meanwhile, for Theodore, Edith was able to fill the emotional void that the death of his mother and Alice had created. She had both his father's intellect and his mother's desire to take care of him.

However, few people knew about the growing relationship between the two. Although they increasingly were seen together at parties and other social events, most thought their companionship was just the renewal of their friendship. Nonetheless, in the winter of 1885, the two became engaged. On November 17, Theodore proposed and Edith eagerly accepted. The engagement was sealed with a ring and a watch. As they had with their budding relationship, Edith and Theodore also kept their engagement secret. During the period, Roosevelt's diary contained entry after entry that had a single letter "E" and no script.

In order to preserve the secrecy of their relationship, the two decided to fulfill a variety of previously arranged obligations and then make a formal announcement. For Theodore, this meant another trip to the West and his Dakota ranches. For Edith, this meant a journey to Europe with her mother and sister. The trio had originally planned to vacation in Europe and then live in Italy, since the cost of living was much lower. With the inheritance from her grandfather, the family could live well in Europe and still maintain their lifestyle. During their time apart, the two wrote each other constantly. As the Roosevelt biographer H. W. Brands states, one particular letter "reveals two distinguishing facets of her personality: her intellectual self-assurance and her emotional insecurity."[15]

Roosevelt understood that Edith would not be happy in the West. She was a product of the Eastern establishment. Therefore he decided to run for the office of mayor of New York City. This would give him employment and a reason to remain in the East. Although he lost the election, it rekindled his interest in politics. He returned to New York where his home at Oyster Bay was renamed "Sagamore Hill" in honor of the Native-American chief (Sagamore Mohannis) who had originally signed the area over to whites. Both Edith and Theodore were very concerned about both the public perception of their relationship and about how the Roosevelt family would react to the engagement. They wanted to wait a "decent" period of time since Theodore

---

[15] Brands, p. 199.

was a recent widower and they did not want to give the appearance of inappropriateness. In addition, there was the question of Bamie. Roosevelt's sister had cared for Alice for the last two years and in many ways had become a surrogate wife for Theodore. In addition to taking care of Baby Lee, Bamie also ran the household and acted as hostess for Theodore. She had few prospects for marriage and the couple was troubled by the idea of forcing her out on her own and separating her from Baby Lee.

Before they were able to announce the news of their engagement on their terms, the *New York Times* published a notice of their forthcoming marriage. Roosevelt's sisters were so surprised that they forced the paper to publish a retraction. Roosevelt tried to explain to his sisters that he had delayed telling them because they had not set a date. Meanwhile, the announcement temporarily soured the friendship between Edith and the Roosevelt sisters. Both seemed to feel that Edith was coming between them and their brother. The news had its greatest impact on Bamie. She was thirty-one and seemed destined to remain a spinster. At the time, Baby Lee appeared to be the closest that Bamie would ever come to having a child of her own. Roosevelt felt an enormous degree of responsibility toward Bamie. Theodore even insisted that Bamie "keep" Baby Lee afer he was married and that he would pay the expenses for her upbringing. For her part, Edith did not want to be perceived as causing problems in the close-knit Roosevelt family. Now that she finally had Theodore, she did not want any external factors to cause trouble for her. To make matters worse, Edith was still in Europe during this episode. The distance heightened Edith's concerns.

Theodore remained sensitive about the marriage announcement. He arranged to have the formal notice published two days after he had set sail for London to meet with Edith. To a certain extent, both Theodore and Edith misjudged their friends and relatives. After the initial shock subsided, most realized that the composed and controlled Edith was the best match for the exuberant Theodore. Within a short period of time, letters and congratulations were pouring in. The goodwill that the engagement generated surprised the couple, but also gave them great satisfaction.

The behavior of the two during this period was seen by many as marked by self-guilt. For Theodore it seems clear that at some level he believed that a remarriage would be a betrayal of his first wife. Meanwhile, Edith was dealing with the dichotomy of the situation. She was marrying Theodore, but she was doing so as his second choice. In the midst of these mental wranglings was

Alice who remained a reminder of the first marriage. In later life, Alice provided her perception of the situation:

> My stepmother was terribly conscientious about me. She had insisted on keeping me with them when they married. My father obviously didn't want the symbol of his infidelity around. His *two* [italics in the original] infidelities, in fact: infidelity to my stepmother by marrying my mother first, and to my mother by going back to my stepmother after she died. It was all so dreadfully Victorian and mixed up. My stepmother added a typically caustic twist by telling my brother Ted, who naturally repeated it to me, that it was just as well that my mother had died when she did because my father would have been bored to death staying married to her. I think she always resented being the second choice and she never really forgave him his first marriage. In many ways she was a very hard woman. She was Jonathan Edwards stock and she had almost a gift for making her own people uncomfortable.[16]

As time went by tensions between Alice and Edith would serve as the main source of emotional discord in the Roosevelt household.

Plans were drawn up for the wedding to take place in London on December 2, 1886. Bamie agreed to accompany Roosevelt to London for the ceremony, but Corrine did not. Edith's younger sister was her bridesmaid and Cecil Spring-Rice, a British diplomat and friend of Roosevelts, served as best-man. Although he had not known Spring-Rice very long, Theodore's positive impressions of the young aristocrat proved to be accurate and he became life-long friends with both bride and groom. Prior to the ceremony, Bamie helped Edith arrange her dress. The wedding was held at St. George's in Hanover Square. After the couple exchanged vows, they held a breakfast for the wedding party and then departed for Dover. From the coast of England, they went to Europe for their honeymoon. Theodore's sensitivity over his first wife remained, and he made sure that the newly-weds did not travel to any of the points that he and Alice had been to on his first honeymoon.

Edith's sister and mother joined the couple in the midst of their fifteen-week journey. Roosevelt seemed to enjoy their company and in fact used their presence as a means to keep Edith occupied while he did some writing. Unromantic as this may sound, there was a real necessity for Roosevelt to earn extra money since he had lost the mayoral race and had no other real source of

---

[16] Micheal Teague, *Mrs. L: Conversations with Alice Roosevelt Longworth* (Garden City, New York: Doubleday & Company, 1981), p. 37.

income. In addition, he had received news that a series of storms had devastated his holdings in the Dakotas. This led Theodore to try to economize on the honeymoon, but such efforts were short-lived and he consistently exceeded even his original budget. For her part, the new wife fully intended to reorganize the Roosevelt household upon their return in order to secure financial security. Meanwhile, Edith did not mind Roosevelt's writing efforts. Since she enjoyed having time to herself and now that she had finally won Theodore, there would be little that could spoil the honeymoon. She even helped Theodore edit the essays. In a letter to his sister, Roosevelt states "I read them all to Edith and her corrections and help were most valuable."[17] About half-way through the honeymoon, Edith became pregnant.

The couple had met Edith's mother and sister in Rome on February 5. The Roosevelts went on to Venice where Edith's pregnancy was discovered. They returned to London, on their way back to the United States. Their final days in London climaxed the honeymoon. The two were able to arrange a meeting with the renowned poet Robert Browning. Edith had been a devoted fan since her youth and quite overwhelmed to meet the great poet. In her later life, Edith would often proclaim that her extended honeymoon was one of the happiest periods of her life.

---

[17] Robinson, p. 128.

Chapter 3

POLITICIAN'S WIFE

When the Roosevelts returned from Europe, in March of 1887, Theodore announced his intention to concentrate on ranching and his burgeoning writing career. He disavowed politics completely, but this pledge would not last. Meanwhile, the first real test of the new couple concerned Baby Lee. Roosevelt had told Bamie that he wished for her to care for Alice before he left for Europe. While the couple was in Europe, Edith surprised Theodore when she insisted that they care for Alice. Roosevelt was very uncomfortable being forced to choose between two of the three most important women in his life. He did not want to hurt Bamie, but the intensity of Edith's feelings made him loathe to deny her this request, especially at this stage of the marriage. He wrote to Bamie that "Edith feels more strongly about her [Alice] than I could have ever imagined."[1]

Fortunately for Theodore, Bamie understood the logic of Edith's position. She agreed to return Baby Lee with little commotion. In return, Bamie would continue to take care of Alice until the summer when she and the baby would join Edith and Theodore at Sagamore Hill and undergo a transition period. Although she agreed with Edith, the episode soured relations between Bamie and Edith. The two remained polite acquaintances, but their friendship never really recovered. Corrine also found that her relationship with Edith suffered. Both sisters discovered that they now had a powerful rival for Theodore's affection in Edith. In the future, access to Theodore would come mainly

---

[1] Theodore Roosevelt to Anna Cowles Roosevelt, January 10, 1887, Theodore Roosevelt Birthplace.

through the consent of Edith. At several points in the years ahead, relations between Edith and the sisters would be tested by jealousy on the part of all parties.

The second major issue to confront the newlyweds centered around Roosevelt's financial stability. Edith had always known that Theodore was a poor financial manager, but upon going over his records, she discovered that the family was in serious economic trouble. To compound matters, storms in the West had seriously damaged Roosevelt's ranches, killing livestock and destroying property. Roosevelt lost approximately 65 percent of his stock and about half of his $85,000 investment. In a calculating fashion that demonstrated the steely-reserve of Edith, she suggested that the family close Sagamore Hill. Short of that drastic step, she ordered immediate reductions in expenses. Through her efficiency as a household manager, Edith was able to reduce expenses by half. Although some social gatherings were curtailed, the new Mrs. Roosevelt also managed to maintain the social obligations of the family.

Edith and Theodore set about arranging Sagamore Hill as a home. They brought in furniture and hung paintings and other accouterments. Theodore insisted on a strongly masculine decor. There were animal-skin rugs and the heads of various animals that had succumbed on Theodore's hunting expeditions. Although the style did not suit Edith's tastes, she demurred to Theodore's fashions. One reason for her acceptance of Theodore's manly interior motif may have been to banish any lingering memories of his departed wife.[2] As time went by and the family's children were born, Alice's presence was never really a factor. For Theodore, it was almost as if his first wife never existed.

As was her habit in life, Edith established a place for herself where she could have her privacy and personal space. Across from Theodore's office, where he wrote and conducted his correspondence, Edith established a parlor. The room was on the first floor and had a view of Oyster Bay. It was simply furnished and the writing desk that had been inherited from her Aunt Kermit, dominated the settings. This room became Edith's personal refuge from the boisterousness of family and husband, as well as the area where she managed the household and family finances.

---

[2] Brands, p. 216.

During that summer, Theodore worked to restore the family's finances by writing. In 1886, Roosevelt had completed a work on the life of Thomas Hart Benton, the noted Senator from Missouri. The work was published by Houghton Mifflin and met with considerable critical and popular success. This was followed by a contract from the publisher for a biography of Gouverneur Morris, the Revolutionary War statesman. Throughout the summer of 1887, Roosevelt worked to complete the manuscript for the Morris work as Edith's pregnancy progressed.

There were few visitors to Sagamore Hill during that summer. Bamie, Corrine and her family and Spring-Rice were the only recorded guests. Edith and Theodore established a daily routine that became commonplace. During the mornings, Edith dealt with correspondence and household management. She often sewed or did other needlework. Meanwhile, Theodore worked on his writings. After lunch, the couple would engage in outdoor activity. They often went for lengthy hikes or horseback rides or went swimming. Rowing remained one of Theodore's favorite endeavors. On many an afternoon, he would row while Edith read aloud. The couple would explore the various marshes and coves around Oyster Bay.

Edith gave birth to a son, Theodore Junior, on September 13 at 2:15 in the morning. While the labor was long, it was uncomplicated and both mother and son emerged healthy, but tired. That both were healthy must have been a great relief to Theodore after the events surrounding the birth of his first child. Within a few months, Edith was active again. By January, he had even taught her the game of tennis. By the spring, she was pregnant once more. Unfortunately, on July 18, 1888, Edith suffered a miscarriage. The miscarriage seems to have dramatically shaken Theodore. Within two weeks he departed on a six-week hunting trip. This pattern of escapism, of running away from problems, had manifested itself in the events surrounding the birth of Alice. This same pattern marked Roosevelt's familial relationships for the rest of his life.

BACK ON THE CAMPAIGN TRAIL

Roosevelt returned from his hunting trip in time to participate in the 1888 presidential campaign. In return for his efforts, his friend Henry Cabot Lodge managed to secure a post for Roosevelt as one of three members of the Federal

Civil Service Commission. Although the pay was low, $3,500, Roosevelt viewed the position as a stepping stone for future advancement. In addition, he enjoyed the work. In his first year on the Commission, he wrote Corrine: "I have hated being so much away from home this summer, but I am very glad I took the place [on the Commission] and I have really enjoyed my work."[3] The Commission had little real power, but it could and did bring to light corruption and wrongdoing in the public sector. Most significantly, it kept Roosevelt in the forefront of public attention. It also helped cement Roosevelt's reputation as a reformer.

By the time Roosevelt assumed his new duties, Edith was pregnant again. His duties kept him in Washington while Edith remained at Sagamore Hill. Alone and pregnant, Edith developed a depression.[4] She felt abandoned by her husband who left her to manage the household and raise the children. To make matters worse, Theodore was still in Washington when his second son, Kermit, was born prematurely on October 10, 1889. In spite of the earlier tensions between the two women, Bamie raced to Oyster Bay to help Edith. In addition to caring for Edith, Bamie even sent off the birth announcements. In December, Bamie volunteered to watch the children, including the newborn, while Edith traveled to Washington, D.C., to help Roosevelt set-up his house. Edith enjoyed Washington. Compared with the bustle of New York, the capital city was at that time relatively small and quiet. She also appreciated the social season in Washington to a far greater degree than she had the social circles of New York City. The aura of power and prestige was particularly appealing. She became friends with such luminaries as the historian Henry Brooks Adams and Henry Cabot Lodge's wife Anna or "Nannie." The children joined their parents just before Christmas.

During this period, Roosevelt was finishing writing a massive historical work, *The Winning of the West*. Edith found that in order to maintain Sagamore Hill and the house in Washington, the family needed an additional $4,000 in income. Hence, he was constantly writing, producing both short books and articles for journals. Volumes one and two of *The Winning of the West* were published in 1889, and they became national best sellers. The Roosevelts' financial predicament improved dramatically.

---

[3] Robinson, p. 133.
[4] Morris, p. 119.

In the fall of 1890, Roosevelt took Edith, his sisters, Cabot Lodge and others on a trip through the West. Edith was an expert horsewoman, and despite her upbringing, she really liked the West. While on the journey, Roosevelt also took them to Yellowstone. After they returned to Washington, Edith was pregnant.

On August 13, 1891, Edith delivered a girl, Ethel. During this and her previous pregnancies, Edith seemed to blossom. The pregnancies did not exert an undue toll on her health and she recovered from the births quickly. Alice was growing into a beautiful young woman, while Theodore Junior or "Ted" had his father's energy and intelligence. On the other hand, Kermit's personality matched that of his mother. He was bookish and introverted. Finally, Ethel also had the energy and drive of Theodore. She was stocky and strong and earned the nickname "Elephant Johnny" from her father who called her "a jolly naughty whacky baby."[5]

Theodore was an affectionate father, but more often than not he was absent. To Edith fell the burden of raising the children. Often when Theodore was present he played with children in such a fashion that it was hard to tell who was the parent and who was the child. Edith had to scold Theodore almost as often as she did the children. In addition, Roosevelt continued to frustrate her efforts to bring the family's budget under control. She tried establishing an allowance for him, but he constantly overspent. For instance, just after the birth of Ethel, Roosevelt again embarked on a six-week hunting trip. The financial situation of the Roosevelts improved slightly in 1892. John Carow, an uncle of Edith's, died and left her an estate which paid an annual income of $1,200. Even with the additional income, the family continued to have monetary problems as Theodore persisted in his extravagant spending habits. He therefore continued to write in order to supplement his income.

POLITICS AS USUAL

During the fall of 1892, Roosevelt campaigned vigorously for incumbent President Benjamin Harrison. Roosevelt's reputation as a reformer led the Republican Party to send him into the West in order to try and gain votes from areas that had supported populist and progressive candidates. Roosevelt had personal as well as ideological reasons for his efforts. Because of the family's financial position, Roosevelt desperately needed his civil service position. Despite the attempts of Roosevelt and the Republicans, Harrison lost the election to Grover Cleveland.

Roosevelt was surprised to learn that Cleveland wanted him to retain his post on the Civil Service Commission. His credentials as a progressive and his performance on the Commission, in which he vigorously worked to expose corruption, had impressed Cleveland. Under new regulations, at least one member of the Civil Service Commission had to be a member of the minority party and the new President preferred that Republican to be Roosevelt.

The young politician had to tread carefully. On the one hand, Roosevelt did need the job and he hoped to retain it long enough for the publication of volumes three and four of *The Winning of the West*. He also enjoyed his time in Washington and genuinely liked being involved in the machinery of government. His job gave him access to many of the most powerful men in the nation. Furthermore, many of his new friends, including Cabot Lodge and Spring-Rice resided in the nation's capital. On the other hand, by working for a Democratic administration, Roosevelt risked any political future he might have with the Republican Party. Although he often told friends and family that he had no intention of seeking elected office again, he confided to Edith that he sought to reenter the "fray." The two discussed the possibility that Roosevelt run for Congress. They concurred that this would be one potential answer to the family's financial woes. Many of the more conservative members of the Republican Party already considered Roosevelt as a radical and too liberal for their tastes, and he was concerned that his service in the Cleveland administration would alienate other members of the Party.

The financial problems of the family were compounded by a series of events in 1893. First, the nation underwent a severe economic depression. Both Edith and Theodore had limited investments and all of these suffered during the period. Second, while Roosevelt's job provided the family's main source of income, it also required that the Roosevelts maintain two homes, the estate at Sagamore Hill and an address in Washington. Most significantly, Edith usually remained at Oyster Bay while Theodore resided in the capital. Besides that obvious strain that the time apart placed on the couple, the distance meant that Edith could not monitor Theodore's spending. While Edith cut back on spending and deftly managed the household in a manner

---

[5] Morris, Edmund, p. 443.

that reduced or at least constrained expenses, Theodore continued to spend at an alarming rate and look to Edith to manage the accounts. Third, and finally, Theodore's brother Elliott was falling apart from the consequences of alcoholism. For several years, Roosevelt and his sisters tried a variety of tactics to help Elliott. They found jobs for him, provided money and sought to help him rehabilitate himself. However, by the summer of 1894, Elliott had reached his end.

Following a series of crises, including a carriage wreck and a series of affairs, Elliott lost his sanity. He ultimately had to be restrained. On August 14, he died from the impact of his lifelong addiction to alcohol. His brother's death dramatically affected Theodore. Edith worried about the long-term impact of the event on her husband. She sought to distract Theodore by involving him more with the family. She knew that when Theodore was around the children, his other cares and worries seemed to vanish and he reverted to a childlike state. His children or "bunnies" as he called them were the source of constant amusement.[6] She also noticed that Theodore did best when he was busy. As long as he had a variety of projects underway, Roosevelt remained happy. However, when there was not much to occupy his time, he had a tendency to become listless and brood on his problems. During the summer of 1894, Roosevelt's main problems continued to revolve around the family's finances and his political future. Meanwhile, Edith was pregnant for a fifth time. Her third son, Archie, was born on April 9.

At the end of that summer, a group of New York Republicans met with Roosevelt and asked him to run for mayor of the city. Public discontent with the corruption in city politics and Roosevelt's popular appeal seemed to mean that the young reformer had a very good chance of winning the election. The position paid well and it would have meant that the family would have been closer to Sagamore Hill. However, Edith was uncomfortable with the idea of Theodore giving-up his secure civil service position in order to engage in a political race that he might not win. Edith worried what might happen if Theodore lost the election and the family was left without a steady income. In addition, like her husband, Edith sincerely enjoyed the social setting in Washington and was loath to leave it.[7] During their marriage, Edith seldom

---

[6] Robinson, p. 156.

[7] Brands, p. 266.

took an adamant stand on issues, but she strenuously opposed Theodore campaigning for the mayorship.

Roosevelt declined the offer to run. Soon afterwards, however, he began to regret his decision. Over the weeks leading up to the election, Roosevelt grew increasingly resentful of Edith's pressure to not seek the office. After another reformist candidate won the election, Roosevelt grew even more bitter. Soon after declining the nomination, Roosevelt left the family for a trip to the Dakotas. For the first time during their marriage, Edith and Theodore underwent a significant crisis in their relationship. Edith deeply regretted her actions and was despondent. She was afraid that Theodore would never forgive her. To compound matters, Corrine and others in the Roosevelt family had counseled Theodore to run.

While Theodore overcame his resentment and forgave Edith, she never forgot the lesson of the episode. Never again would she attempt to persuade her husband to not seek a certain office. On more than one occasion she expressed her opinion that she thought he should not run for a particular office, but she never again offered the level of opposition that she did over the mayoral race. Most significantly, although Theodore continued to seek Edith's advice and counsel, he increasingly came to rely more on his sisters for political recommendations. Edith would resent this habit throughout their marriage.

Recognizing how distraught Edith was, Bamie took her and the children to Vermont. Meanwhile Theodore returned to New York and decided to seek a government position in either the city or state. He hoped to use a position in the state as a springboard for higher office. The new mayor offered Roosevelt an appointment as the commissioner of street cleaning–a position Roosevelt immediately refused. After being in the national spotlight, Roosevelt wanted a position of some stature. Ultimately he was offered a position as one of four police commissioners. Roosevelt gladly accepted the post.

The police position offered a variety of advantages for the Roosevelts. The pay was $6,000 per year, far more than his federal appointment, and it carried with it a great deal of public exposure. Roosevelt would be in the public eye as he battled to end graft and corruption in the police department. Soon after being appointed, Roosevelt was elected by his fellow commissioners as president of the commission. Roosevelt ultimately instituted a variety of reforms that were both effective and popular. For instance, he established a bicycle squad that was able to respond to crimes quickly. After one year of operation, the squad had made over a thousand arrests.[8] Roosevelt himself rode a bicycle to and from work and often roamed the streets at night in a one-man crusade to ensure that police officers did their duty. These antics were extremely popular and the public quickly perceived that Roosevelt was a workaholic and a genuine reformer.

The family's finances were better, especially with the publication of the remaining volumes of *The Winning of the West*, and the increase in pay. Although he was geographically closer to Edith and the family, Roosevelt's hours kept him from the family. In April of 1895, Edith received word that her mother had died in Italy. While she had not been close with Gertrude, she felt guilt at not being with her at the end. Following Gertrude's death, Edith invited her sister to Sagamore Hill. Emily remained at the family's residence for six months, but by the end, she and Edith had begun to quarrel. The emotional strain of her mother's death followed by the difficult period with her sister, on top of caring for the five children, left Edith emotionally exhausted. More importantly, Edith began to suffer some health problems. Whether from the physical strain of having four children within a relatively short period of time or from the emotional strain of the past year, she began to suffer migraines.

Nonetheless, by 1896, Edith was truly happy and comfortable in her role as mother and political wife. At thirty-four, Edith was in the midst of one of the more satisfying times of her life. While Theodore scourged the streets of New York, Edith was left to supervise and care for the rambunctious children. Her self-confidence and calm manner helped deal with the high-spirited children who were often in various degrees of trouble. Edith had Alice and Ted enrolled with the same dance instructor that she had as a girl, and in the fall, Ted entered Cove Neck School. Although, Alice had begun to develop her own character, she had not reached the point of open rebellion as she would later.

Theodore campaigned hard for the election of William McKinley in 1896 and lobbied equally as hard for an appointment as Assistant Secretary of the Navy. McKinley won the election and after some additional campaigning by Roosevelt and his friends, including Cabot Lodge, on April 6, 1897, Roosevelt received word of his new appointment. Although the move to Washington would require another disruption and relocation of the family, Edith was

---

[8] Ibid, p. 280.

happy to be returning to her Washington friends and the society of the capital. In addition, the new appointment would mean another increase in pay. Theodore wrote to his friend Spring-Rice that "I have never seen her [Edith] so well as she was this winter, in looks, in health in spirits and everything."[9]

Soon after Roosevelt's appointment, tension between the United States and Spain over Cuba began to reach the crisis level. Roosevelt himself "became convinced that the war would come"[10] and worked energetically to ensure it. The Secretary of the Navy was the aging politician John D. Long who seemed pleased that he had an energetic assistant who could fulfill both his and his superior's office. While Roosevelt wrote essays in support of war and worked to convince politicians to support an aggressive stance toward Spain, Edith found herself pregnant again. This slowed the move from New York to Washington. Theodore moved to the capitol and began his war campaign, while Edith continued to care for the children. She traveled to the capital in August to help him arrange a rented house, but did not formally move to Washington until October when the weather was cooler. Upon her arrival in the capital, the eight-month pregnant Edith immediately began to put the family's affairs in order. Kermit and Archie were enrolled at a public school and she began to try to put the family's finances in order after Theodore had spent several months on his own destroying them. On November 9, Edith delivered their fifth child and fourth son, Quentin.

Unlike her previous deliveries which were relatively uncomplicated, with Quentin, Edith developed postpartum health problems. Initially, she was believed to have grippe, an abdominal disease with flu-like symptoms, but subsequently she was diagnosed with an abscess which was causing an abdominal infection. Roosevelt at one point was terrified because he became convinced that she had typhoid (the same disease which killed his mother). Edith had a recurring fever for four weeks and headaches so sever that she could not read or write. Roosevelt sent the children to various relatives and friends and tried to both care for his wife and maintain the demands of his office. The specter of the death of his first wife haunted Roosevelt and even though doctors recommended surgery, he was terrified of the possibility. On March 5, a gynecologist operated and removed the abscess. Through the ordeal, it was difficult to say who helped whom the most. Theodore was

---

[9] Theodore Roosevelt to Cecil Rice-Spring, May 29, 1897; Morrison.

[10] Roosevelt, *Autobiography*, p 227.

almost distraught with worry, and in many respects, although she was seriously ill, Edith provided the emotional strength that allowed the couple to get through the ordeal. For instance, Roosevelt described Edith's behavior leading up to the operation as such: "She behaved heroically; quiet, and even laughing, while I held her hand until the ghastly preparations had been made."[11] Her recovery took several months. For a period, the wound had to remain open so that it could be drained.

In the midst of Edith's illness, Roosevelt found himself torn between caring for his wife and preparing for war. On February 15, 1898, the U.S. battleship the *Maine* exploded and sank in the harbor of Havana, Cuba. As a result of the explosion, 264 American sailors were killed. Roosevelt and many other hawks urged war. However, it would not be until April 11, before McKinley asked Congress for a declaration of war. During this period, Roosevelt worked to secure some kind of commission in the Army. Although Edith, who was still recovering, and Roosevelt's friends and family tried to discourage him, he accepted a commission as a lieutenant colonel in a volunteer cavalry unit.[12]

---

[11]Theodore Roosevelt to Anna (Bamie) Roosevelt Cowles, March 7, 1898; Morrison, I, p. 790.

[12] Roosevelt was initially offered full command of a cavalry regiment, but because of his inexperience with the military he asked to be placed under the command of his friend Colonel Leonard Wood.

Chapter 4

ON THE HOME FRONT

As Theodore prepared to go to war, Edith remained weak and was still recovering from her recent surgery. That Theodore would leave her at this stage must have been deeply troubling. In addition to her own physical problems, the family was in the midst of another crisis over Ted's health. Ted had begun to have severe headaches. A succession of doctors was unable to diagnose a physical reason for the headaches. Eventually one doctor, who was close to the family and therefor had more insight on the nature of the household, spoke at some length with Edith. After the discussion, he announced that he concurred with a suggestion that Edith had made. Ted's headaches were the result of stress caused by the pressure his father put on him to excel in sports, academics and character.[1] Theodore initially resisted the diagnosis, but under pressure from Edith, he ultimately tried to tone down his expectations.

The climax of Ted's problems occurred simultaneously with Edith's illness and the boy was sent to live with Bamie in New York for a period. Away from the demands of his father, Ted did well. The atmosphere at Bamie's house, away from both parental pressure and the strain of witnessing his mother's recovery, provided the perfect recovery setting. Tension between Alice and her parents had also begun to reach a serious level during this period. Alice would later state that Edith "was a pleasure and I was devoted to her. You couldn't match her for all kinds of things and we shared many of the same interests, especially literature. It was said that in some respects I was

---

[1] Brands, p. 336.

more like her than her own children."[2] During the summer, Alice had refused to be confirmed in the church and then also refused to be sent to a boarding school in New York. She employed a variety of threats and other tactics to avoid the school. She asserted "that if the family insisted, and sent me, I should do something dreadful." In addition, she ensured that "every afternoon I made a point of crying about it."[3] Edith and Theodore relented and instead employed a governess for her early education.

The actions and conditions of both Alice and Ted certainly weighed heavily on Edith's mind as Theodore cheerfully prepared for his new adventure. There was also the very real possibility that Theodore could be injured or killed. On the practical level, Edith faced the prospect of raising six children on limited means. Theodore did have some insurance, but it is questionable as to whether he had prepared for the family's economic future should something happen to him. On another level, Edith deeply loved her husband and his loss would be devastating to both her and the children. That he would leave in the midst of this succession of family crises, including her illness, must have wounded Edith. Her husband's cavalier attitude toward her and the family was also distressing.

On the one hand, Roosevelt expressed sentiments that were common at the time. In his autobiography he states that "I had always felt that if there were a serious war I wished to be in a position to explain to my children why I did take part in it, and not why I did not take part in it."[4] Yet he also displayed a callousness toward his family. Years later, he summarized his feelings in a letter to his friend Archie Butt:

> When the chance came for me to go to Cuba with the Rough Riders Mrs. Roosevelt was very ill and so was Teddy. It was a question if either would ultimately get well. You know what my wife and children mean to me; yet I made up my mind that I would not allow even a death to stand in my way; that it was my one chance to do something for my country and for my family and my one chance to cut my little notch on the stick that stands as a measuring-rod in every family. I know now that I would have turned from my wife's deathbed to have answered that call.[5]

---

[2] Teague, p. 36.

[3] Alice Roosevelt Longworth, *Crowded Hours: Reminiscences of Alice Roosevelt Longworth* (New York, Charles Scribner's Sons, 1933), p. 26.

[4] Roosevelt, *Autobiography*, p. 237.

[5] Archibald W. Butt, *Letters,* ed. Lawrence F. Abbot (New York: Doubleday, 1924), p. 146.

While Theodore's attitude toward the family pained Edith and reinforced where she stood on his list of priorities, she had learned her lesson from the mayoral campaign. As she would do in the future, Edith expressed her opinions to Theodore on why he should not go, but once she saw that his mind was made-up, she offered her full support. Although she was still recovering from her illness, Edith went to social events with Theodore during the last few weeks before he left and generally tried to help take care of the numerous minor tasks necessary before he departed. For his part, Theodore endeavored to spend as much time with Edith and the children as possible, even though it meant that he joined his regiment later than the other officers.

SOLDIER'S WIFE

While Theodore's regiment, the self-proclaimed Rough Riders, underwent training in the West, Edith and her husband carried on a lively correspondence. Edith would read portions of his letters to the children and recount their comments and experiences to her husband in her letters. The Rough Riders were sent to Tampa, Florida in preparation for the invasion of Cuba. Edith was fully recovered by now, and made arrangements to travel to Tampa to be with Theodore before he embarked on the invasion. She arrived on June 1, 1898. Theodore had arranged to stay with Edith at the Tampa Bay Hotel and had been granted permission to spend his nights with his wife. Edith met Theodore's fellow officers and though she understood the potential risks of his service, she also realized that her husband was in his element. His energy and enthusiasm made him both popular and effective with his fellow officers and the troops. Roosevelt had learned a considerable amount from his friend Leonard Wood, the commander of the Rough Riders, and had become a first rate officer. Although parting from her husband was difficult, Edith appreciated the time in Tampa for the insights that it provided on her husband's character. For his part, Theodore's feelings were succinctly summed up in a letter to his children: "It has been a real holiday to have darling mother here."[6]

---

[6] Theodore Roosevelt to "Blessed Bunnies" (his children), June 6, 1898, Theodore Roosevelt, *Theodore Roosevelt's Letters to his Children*, ed. Joseph Bucklin Bishop (New York: Charles Scribner's Sons, 1919), p. 13.

Like countless other American wives during the war, Edith nervously awaited news of the war. On June 14, eight days after she left to return to New York, the American invasion fleet left for Cuba. The actual invasion was anticlimactic and the American troops initially met little resistence when they landed in Cuba. Roosevelt's letters to Edith and the rest of the family had two distinguishing traits. They tended to downplay the physical danger that he was in. His accounts of battle minimized the death and carnage of combat. Concurrently, however, he described in great detail the horrid living conditions of the campaign. In one letter he informed Edith that his personal bags, which included his toiletry items and extra clothes, had been lost. In another, he went so far as to describe the vultures that were feasting on the dead following one engagement.[7]

During the invasion, Wood was promoted to brigade commander and Roosevelt was given command of the Rough Rider Regiment. The climatic battle of the operation in Cuba was the Battle of San Juan Heights. In this engagement, Roosevelt distinguished himself by personally leading his men in an assault against first Kettle Hill and then San Juan Hill. For his actions, Roosevelt was promoted to full colonel and recommended for the Medal of Honor. His actions were widely reported in the press and he was perceived as one of the main heroes of the war by the public. Roosevelt encouraged the dramatic accounts of his bravery and was not modest about his part in the campaign. Immediately after the Battle of San Juan Hill, Roosevelt declared "I think I earned my Colonelcy and medal of honor, and hope I get them."[8] He tried to explain his heroism in the context of his family and his place in history in a letter to his friend Henry Cabot Lodge

> I hope you will not think I grumble too much or am too much worried; it is not the least for myself; I am more than satisfied even though I die of yellow fever tomorrow, for at least I feel that I have done something which enables me to leave a name to the children of which they can rightly be proud and which will serve in some sense as a substitute for not leaving them more money.[9]

---

[7] Morrison, 2, p. 845.

[8] Theodore Roosevelt to Henry Cabot Lodge, July 10, 1898, quoted in Brands, p. 356.

[9] Theodore Roosevelt to Henry Cabot Lodge, July 19, 1898; quoted in Brands, p. 356.

Roosevelt also reveled in the adoration of his men. The close-relationship between him and the Rough Riders would continue throughout his lifetime. Writing to Cabot Lodge, Roosevelt asserted that he was

> Deeply touched by the way the men of the regiment trust and follow me. I think they know I would do anything for them, and when we got into the darkest days I fared precisely as they did. Certainly in battle or in the march or in the trenches I never went anywhere but I found them eager to follow me. I was not reckless; but with a regiment like this, and indeed I think with most regiments, the man in command must take all the risks which he asks his men to take if he is going to get the best work out of them. On the day of the big fight I had to ask my men to do a deed that European military writers consider utterly impossible of performance, that is, to attack over open ground unshaken infantry armed with the best modern repeating rifles behind a formidable system of entrenchments. The only way to get them to do it in the way it had to be done was to lead them myself.[10]

On the home front, Edith had stayed at Sagamore Hill with the children over the summer. She was both proud and relieved as accounts of the battle were published in the papers. Roosevelt's conduct pleased her, although she worried that he was taking unnecessary risks. She understood her husband's psychological need to prove himself in battle, but felt that he discounted his importance to her and the family. While Theodore distinguished himself in Cuba, Edith continued to manage the family's accounts and raise the children.

She looked forward to her husband's return, but was unsettled by the calls that had already begun to sweep across newspaper editorial pages for Theodore to seek public office. Most significantly, talk had already begun to surface that upon his return, Roosevelt should run for governor of New York. Even members of the Democratic Party began to line-up in support of his candidacy. As the fighting wound down, she was pleased that Roosevelt had done well, but had not been seriously wounded. He had been slightly wounded by shrapnel in his arm, however the wound was minor.

After the Battle of San Juan Hill, coupled with American successes in the invasion of Puerto Rico and the Philippines, the Spanish asked that negotiations be opened with Washington. Over the course of the final few weeks of the war, Roosevelt worked to get his troops evacuated from Cuba while the peace negotiations between Washington and Madrid were ongoing.

---

[10] Ibid; p. 357.

The heat and humidity combined with tropical diseases to exact a great toll on the American forces in Cuba. The camps were not very sanitary and Roosevelt bemoaned the lack of hygiene and the inefficiency of the War Department in providing adequate supplies for the troops. In a letter to his sister Corrine and her husband he concluded with the phrase that "the mismanagement has been beyond belief."[11]

Edith was concerned that Theodore might contract yellow fever or malaria, but on August 15, she received a message that Roosevelt and his troops had been returned to Camp Wickoff at Mantouk, New York. She traveled to the base, only to be told that the entire facility was quarantined because of yellow fever. As she had often done in the past, Edith demonstrated her indefatigability. She arranged to have Theodore smuggled out of camp for a short period of time by convincing the officer on duty to "look the other way" while her husband slipped out. After their reunion, she stayed in a Red Cross hut, before moving the next day to a nearby house. Taking any opportunity to see Theodore or at least be in the camp with her husband, Edith volunteered to help in the camp hospital. For four days she tended the wounded and sick in spite of the potential for contracting diseases such as yellow fever and typhoid.[12] On August 20, Roosevelt was finally granted a four-day leave.

The couple returned to Sagamore Bay, but found themselves mobbed by crowds both on the journey home and at their house. People surrounded the yard. Some simply wanted to see the "colonel" while others took photographs or souvenirs from the grounds. To a closely guarded person such as Edith these intrusions were completely intolerable. She truly did not understand the public's fascination with her husband and her family. Only with time would Edith come to accept the ramifications of Theodore's visibility and both the media's and public's enchantment with the Roosevelt clan of Oyster Bay. Edith was particularly bothered by the photographers whom she felt significantly infringed on the family's privacy. She was also uncomfortable when reporters attempted to interview the children as they played around the estate. This experience, combined with her natural shyness and aversion to publicity, would color her relations with the press as her husband's political star began to rise.

---

[11] Robinson, p. 176.

[12] Morris, pp. 183-84.

THE POLITICAL COMEBACK

There seemed to be almost universal support for a Roosevelt run for the governorship, but the war hero initially acted quite recalcitrant. When a representative of New York's Republican political boss, Senator Thomas Platt, met with Roosevelt he was noncommital at first. Edith would have preferred that he not run and made these sentiments clear. However, she also made sure that Roosevelt understood she would support him if he chose to run. Since the colonel had been offered a variety of contracts to write about his experiences during the war, Edith emphasized the financial incentives to stay out of politics. Roosevelt could very easily have a career as a writer, at least for the foreseeable future.

Nonetheless, the lure of office was too much for Roosevelt, especially in light of his popularity across the state. On September 14, he met with Republican leaders and agreed to run. At this point, previous efforts to save money came back to haunt Roosevelt, albeit briefly. For several years he had claimed residence in Washington in order to avoid the heavy taxes of New York. This made him technically ineligible to run since he had not been a resident of the state for the minimum five-year period. However, the Party essentially sidestepped the issue when Elihu Root, future Secretary of State under Roosevelt, asserted at the state convention that there were multiple definitions for "residence" and no one challenged the contention. On October 3, the family was notified that Roosevelt had received the Republican nomination. Edith began to prepare for either victory or loss in the upcoming election. She ended the family's lease on the house in Washington–if Theodore won the election, they would stay at the governor's mansion and if he lost the family would simply remain at Sagamore Hill. In spite of the campaign, she also insisted that Theodore accept a number of the proposed offers to publish accounts of his service during the war. If elected, Theodore would be paid $10,000 a year, and with other income and the steps she had already taken, the family would be financially sound for the first time since their marriage.

While Edith was not entirely happy with the campaign and the prospects of her husband's reentry into politics, after she attended his acceptance speech at Carnegie Hall on October 15, 1898, she reported that was "glad" that she had attended and was impressed by the "enthusiasm."[13] And enthusiasm abounded during the campaign. Roosevelt drew large crowds wherever he spoke. While many of his issues did not resonate with the voters, his personality did appeal to the people. Roosevelt was a tireless campaigner, but he made many mistakes during his run. He initially surrounded himself with former soldiers from his regiment, however, after a number of verbal misstatements and other gaffs, he was forced recognize that they were a liability. He conducted the final weeks of the campaign without them.

The Roosevelt family rallied behind the campaign. Corrine and her husband worked on Theodore's behalf. Edith and Alice worked with Roosevelt's secretary to deal with campaign correspondence and write letters on his behalf. Edith turned one of the upstairs rooms into an unofficial campaign headquarters. She also played the political wife and oversaw the management of the household and family while Theodore campaigned. Bamie was unable to do much to help her brother. At the age of forty-three, she had become pregnant. On October 18, Edith received word that Bamie had gone into labor. By the time she got to New York, Bamie had delivered a boy, without serious complications. Edith remained with Bamie for the next three days and then returned to continue her efforts for her husband's campaign.[14]

As election day drew near, the race was extremely close. The election turned out to be one of the closest gubernatorial races in New York history. Of the 1.3 million votes cast, Roosevelt won by a mere eighteen thousand. After the initial euphoria wore off, Edith began to plan the transition and move to the governor's mansion, while Theodore began to plan his administration. Edith traveled to Albany, New York to tour the mansion and met with the outgoing first lady of the state. She found the experience so satisfying and helpful, that as first lady of the United States, Edith would initiate this practice. The mansion was large and roomy. It would be much better than the rented house in Washington.

Before the inauguration, the Roosevelt family spent some time with Bamie and her newborn son. By the time the Roosevelts reached Albany, Edith had contracted the flu. This made the first few days of her time in the capitol difficult. She felt drained and devoid of her usual energy and drive and

---

[13] Edith Kermit Roosevelt to Emily Carow, October 7, 1898, Theodore Roosevelt Collection, Harvard.

[14] Morris, p. 188.

had a difficult time dealing with the variety of ceremonies and maintaining her eye on the children. However, her childhood friend Fanny Smith, now married, also lived in Albany and the two became reacquainted. This brightened her first few days in the state capital. The inauguration ceremony was tiring for Edith, who was still suffering from influenza. However, she came up with a novel approach to relieve the task of having to shake hands with the estimated 5,000 guests: she held bouquets of flowers in both hands. This practice was so successful, without making her appear aloof or stand-offish, that Edith would continue the habit as both wife of the vice-president and as first lady of the United States. The ceremonies took a lot out of Edith and she spent almost a week in bed as she recovered. Once she felt sufficiently well, Edith began the tasks of reorganizing the mansion to meet their tastes and integrating the family into their new lifestyle.

Chapter 5

THE GOVERNOR'S MANSION

While her husband launched himself into a number of political battles that would later significantly impact his career, Edith set about the tasks of managing the move into the governor's mansion and overseeing the family's transition to life in Albany. Her first priorities where to redecorate the house and establish routines for the children. She soon encountered difficulties and complications from a variety of quarters.

Edith's desire to redecorate the governor's mansion was based on both practical and aesthetic concerns. With six children, especially children with the energy and vitality of the Roosevelts, she realized that the stately mansion needed immediate redesigns to accommodate her brood. The mansion had nine bedrooms, but with the children, this did not provide much extra space for the expected number of overnight guests. She turned several rooms which had been cloakrooms or storage areas into bedrooms. She also converted space into a schoolroom for the children that would remain in the house and receive their education there. Finally, to establish an outlet for her husband's energy, she transformed a billiards room in the upstairs into a gym for Theodore to work-out his frustrations and maintain his physical well-being.

When Theodore was elected, the term of office for the governor of the state of New York was only two years. This meant that there had been a number of occupants in the governor's mansion through the years. Each first family had brought their own style and tastes into the house and add their own personal touches. With so many unrelated items and so much furniture, the Roosevelts felt that the house had a cold and impersonal air. Writing to his friend Spring Rice, Roosevelt described the house thus: "We have a great big house which is very comfortable, although in appearance and furnishing, painfully suggestive of that kind of elegance which one sees in a swell Chicago hotel or in the broad room of the directors of some big railway."[1]

The new First Lady of the state of New York also endeavored to transform the mansion from the polyglot collection of furniture and decor of those who had come before into some kind of coherent style. Through the years, chairs, tables and other accouterments that had been given as gifts or purchased had been split apart as one room or another needed a particular item. One of her first acts was to go through the house and return items to the collections where they belonged. Those groups of furniture which were no longer functional or were outdated or were simply beyond the tastes of the Roosevelts were removed and put into storage. Edith also went through the storage areas of the house and reclaimed various items that had been packed away and returned them to display. These included a marble bust and other ornaments.[2]

The state provided all governors with $3,000 annually for repairs and to redecorate the executive mansion, and Roosevelt cheerfully turned the money over to Edith to do with as she pleased. Edith used these funds and some personal monies to purchase new paintings. She seemed to really enjoy her efforts at interior design and after being denied any significant influence over the decor at Sagamore Hill, saw the mansion as a home where she could put more of her stamp and therefore minimize the overtly masculine tastes of her husband. In the end, Edith was able to give the governor's mansion a much more contemporary look while at the same time she increased the functionality of the mansion.

Upon moving to Albany, Edith had to make new arrangements for the care and education of the children. Because of the past experience in trying to get Alice to attend school, it was decided that she would continue to be overseen by an English governess, as would Ethel. The younger boys, Quentin and Archie, would be placed under the care of Mary Ledwith, known as "Mame" to the Roosevelt children. Mame was an Irish nurse who had been originally employed when Edith and Theodore had first been married. The two older boys, Ted and Kermit, were sent to the Albany Military Academy. With considerable domestic help, Edith had more free time than she had enjoyed since their marriage. She used the time to read, work on the house and become

---

[1] Theodore Roosevelt to Cecil Spring-Rice, February 14, 1899, Morrison.
[2] Morris, p. 193.

involved in a number of social and charitable activities in Albany. She also occasionally took a train to New York or Washington to spent time with friends or attend the theater.

Edith also had to oversee the movement of other "members" of the family to the mansion. While she was not overly enthusiastic about pets, Edith had to contend with Theodore's absolute passion about the creatures. Roosevelt insisted that he encouraged the children to have pets as a means to teach them not to be cruel to the weak, but it was very clear to all that the elder Roosevelt enjoyed simply playing with the family's various animals as much as the children did. Theodore acquired first one and then a second pony. There was a virtual menagerie of dogs that ranged from thoroughbreds to mixed breeds which Theodore called "Heinz pickles"–dogs of 57 different breeds. Often these dogs were obtained while Theodore was on hunting trips.[3] The family also had guinea pigs and rabbits. Edith preferred small house dogs as pets, but often found the family's various homes overrun with a variety of species. The movement to Albany meant the corresponding movement of the growing Roosevelt Zoo. Unfortunately for Edith, as time went by the zoo would only increase.

As First Lady of the state of New York, Edith realized that the family needed to present to the public a dignified and refined image. She also believed that the Roosevelts should be portrayed as a close-knit and intimate family. To accomplish this, in light of the rambunctiousness of the children, Edith began to endeavor to manage the image of the family. She made a general rule that the children were not allowed to speak to the press when unsupervised (a rule that would remain when the family moved to Washington). She also sought to cultivate friendships and the favor of the press. For instance, when articles appeared that she liked, Edith would write the reporter a brief thank-you note. An example of this would be the December 1901 letter to a reporter for the *Oyster Bay Pilot*:

> Thank you so much for the article. I think you know quite well what to say that is right, and I am glad to have the little record of the busy Christmas to lay away for the children when they are old. I am so glad you are well and strong again.

---

[3] Joan Paterson Kerr, *A Bully Father: Theodore Roosevelt's Letters to His Children* (New York: Random House, 1995), pp. 28-30.

The Governor and the children join me in best wishes for your happiness and success in the coming year.[4]

Edith also cultivated specific reporters by inviting them to special functions and thereby ensuring that members of the press understood that those who were in her favor were much more likely to have access to her and her husband. Edith's appreciation of the powers and capabilities of the press would serve her well when she became First Lady.

During this period, Edith had to confront a number of tensions within the family. Her most pressing concern was Alice. Her stepdaughter had what could best be described as a "mischievous nature." The emotional impact of her father's distance and the often volatile relationship with Edith combined with Alice's headstrong personality and the natural rebelliousness of adolescence to produce an ongoing series of conflicts between Alice and her parents. Alice's growing interest and appeal to the opposite sex was troublesome for her parents. Meanwhile Alice was bored with Albany. After spending her life in New York and Washington, she found the state capitol dull and lifeless. She described her new surroundings in the following manner:

> Going from Oyster Bay to Albany when father was made governor was anti-climatic. The Executive Mansion there was a hideous building with dreary dark furniture and a funeral air . . . . The atmosphere of the town was pure Trollope. It even had a very Anglican bishop who wore gaiters, a three-cornered hat, and had a dog named Cluny.[5]

Whenever she had the chance, Alice would "escape" to New York where she preferred the company of her Aunt Corrine to life in Albany.[6] Years later Alice would assert that one of the most memorable events that happened to her in Albany "was having most of my teeth loosened when a girl in dancing class kicked me, quite unintentionally I suppose, in the jaw. I later developed abscesses and had to go to hospital in New York for quite awhile."[7]

---

[4] Edith Roosevelt to Amy Cheney, December 15, 1901, in Albert Loren Cheney, *Personal Memoirs of the Home Life of the Late Theodore Roosevelt* (Washington, D.C.: Cheney Publishing, 1919), p. 84.

[5] Teague, p. 54.

[6] Longworth, p. 30.

[7] Teague, p. 54.

Edith's sister Emily also caused her some degree of consternation. After Theodore's election, Emily wrote Edith that she would be willing to come over from Italy and "help" her sister manage the household at the governor's mansion. Edith surmised that Emily wished to ingratiate herself into the family now that Theodore had begun to have financial and political success. In several harshly worded letters, Edith rejected her sister's offer in no uncertain terms and Emily remained in Italy.[8]

Ever since her opposition to Theodore's mayoral bid, Edith found that her husband relied on his sisters for political advice and counsel to a far greater degree than he relied on her. This facet of their marriage was dramatically underscored while Roosevelt was governor. New York politics at that time continued to be dominated by machine politics. The Republican Party machine remained under the control of Platt and Roosevelt had to walk a fine line as governor. ON the one hand, he earnestly sought to reform government and the state's civil service. As such, he often clashed with Platt over appointments to state office since Platt sought to control these jobs so they could be handed out as rewards for supporters or the family members of political allies. Roosevelt tried to make appointments or policy on the basis of merit and this led to fundamental clashes between the two. On the other hand, Roosevelt needed Platt's support to both pass legislation and retain public approval. He also could not alienate the party boss if he wanted to run again for the governorship.

Roosevelt established the habit of meeting Platt at the residence of his sisters. Initially this was done at Bamie's house, but after she moved, Roosevelt arranged to have the meetings at Corrine's home. Often while Edith had breakfast upstairs with the children Roosevelt and one of his sisters would entertain Platt and his political entourage downstairs. Inevitably at some point during the morning, Roosevelt, Platt and first Bamie and then Corrine, would retire to another room to discuss politics and work-out compromises and arrangements. Roosevelt explained the presence of either sister, by asserting that the sibling took such an interest in politics that it would be impolite to exclude her since it was her home. In truth Roosevelt invited his sisters to these meetings to make Platt uncomfortable and to constrain the conversations since he knew that there were some topics the Senator would not discuss in

---

[8] Morris, p. 193-94.

the presence of others. Of course, his sisters also provided a friendly witness to the discussions.[9]

These meetings reinforced the feelings of alienation that Edith felt when it came to her husband's political career. Over and over, it seemed as if she was to be punished or at least reminded of her ill-received counsel at the early stage of Theodore's political career. The meetings also reminded Edith of the close bond between her husband and his sisters and must have stirred some degree of jealousy on the part of Bamie and Corrine.

RUMBLINGS ON THE HORIZON

As the summer of their first year in Albany approached, Edith felt happier and more comfortable with her life than she had in years. In spite of Theodore's political connections with his sisters and Alice's teenage rebelliousness, life was good for the First Lady of New York. Her health had been restored and, with the exception of Alice, the family enjoyed living in Albany. Although she disliked politics, Edith hoped that her husband would be reelected for several more terms after the end of his first two-year stint as governor. She even began to plan for Alice social debut in the near future–a social event that Edith herself had been denied as a youth. Theodore's salary as governor and the success of a series of articles on his experiences during the Spanish-American War had dramatically improved the family's financial status. In addition, Roosevelt's essays were collected in a book, *The Rough Riders*, whose publication brought further income. After years of budgetary concerns and efforts to keep the family solvent, Edith found herself free to entertain in the style that she and Theodore had experienced in their youth.

During the first year at Albany, Edith had really begun to emerge from her habitual reclusiveness. Although she disliked crowds, she increasingly appeared in public with Theodore at ceremonies and official functions. In addition to the annual funds that she could draw from the state for renovations on the governor's mansion, the state also paid the wages of the cooks and servants that worked at the executive mansion. Hence, for the first time since her childhood, Edith had a regular, full staff to do the cleaning and cooking. It was partially because of this staff that the Roosevelts were able to employ two governesses for the children.

---

[9] Robinson, p. 186.

Edith also became engaged in the community in Albany. While she had always had a small circle of close friends, Edith began to entertain more and more people at the governor's mansion. Many of her friends and relatives would later recount that this seemed to be the happiest period of her life. Roosevelt wrote Edith's sister Emily that "Edith is thoroughly enjoying the position of governor's wife."[10]

Theodore was enormously happy as governor. His reputation as a reformer was enhanced as he strove for the passage of a variety of progressive legislation and he had established some degree of independence for himself from the political bosses of the Republican Party. Furthermore, in June of 1899, he toured the country as part of a Rough Riders reunion. During the tour he was received by large crowds and talk began to surface over the possibility of national office. Finally, it had been decided that the family would spend the summer at Oyster Bay and Theodore had pledged to take at least a month's vacation.

The two engaged in many of the activities that had marked their youth, including rowing and hiking through the woods of the estate. Edith spent her mornings tending to the children and her correspondence, while Theodore worked on his latest literary project, a biography of Oliver Cromwell. The afternoons were spent in the outdoors. In the evenings, the parents would read to the children. It was to all accounts a glorious summer.

The year was capped off by the couple's thirteenth wedding anniversary. Theodore had found that is was extremely difficult to purchase presents for his wife. Instead of preparing lists, Edith was of the opinion that if one knew her really well, they would instinctively know her likes and dislikes. Edith had peculiar tastes when it came to gifts. She preferred things that many people might consider to be odd. Among her favorite presents through the years were "decorative moccasins, a tiny gold Aztec frog, [and] an antique pewter sardine server."[11] For their anniversary, Theodore purchased an expensive diamond-backed watch. It was one of his wife's favorite presents and she made a habit of wearing it constantly.

As so often happened during her lifetime, just as life reached a comfortable pattern, there were events on the horizon which would dramatically alter the Roosevelt family. Roosevelt's friends began circulating

---

[10] Theodore Roosevelt to Emily Carow, March 20, 1899, Morrison.

[11] Morris, p. 201.

the idea that he might replace the incumbent Vice President Garret Hobart during the presidential election in 1900. Henry Cabot Lodge seems to have been one of the principal proponents of this notion. By this point in his career, Roosevelt had developed aspirations to be president, although he did not share this ambition with Edith. McKinley's popularity more or less assured him reelection as president in 1900. The central question for Roosevelt then became, what was the optimum way to position himself for a run for the presidency in 1904, at which point McKinley would have served two terms and would surely retire as custom dictated.

Roosevelt's continuing difficulties with New York political boss Platt left his future in some doubt in the state. Platt had made it clear that he would have liked to rid himself of the reformist governor. This made Theodore and Edith apprehensive because Platt had the political clout to deny Roosevelt the Republican nomination for the governor's office in 1900. However, Roosevelt was popular and well-regarded by most of the state, and to deny him a second bid would cost Platt an enormous amount of political capital. Therefore Platt was working to get rid of Roosevelt by moving him to a different office, preferably one outside of the state of New York. In addition to conjecture about the vice-presidency, other potential posts for Roosevelt that were being speculated about included that of secretary of war or even governor-general of the Philippines.

When discussion of the vice-presidency reached Edith's ears, she came out forcefully against it. She genuinely liked Albany and was comfortable with her husband's role as governor. She was also politically astute enough to realize that Theodore could be easily reelected in the upcoming gubernatorial campaign and that Platt would not sacrifice his machine to stop the reelection bid. She also realized that while the vice-presidency might be a stepping stone to the presidency it could also be the end of her husband's career. Not since Martin Van Buren followed Andrew Jackson had a sitting vice president succeeded a president by being elected. Finally, there were financial considerations. The governorship of New York actually paid more than the vice-presidency and the vice president did not have the same expense reimbursement as did the governor. These considerations seemed to sway Roosevelt and as he prepared for his second year in office, he let it be known that he intended to seek another term as governor.

In the midst of these political wranglings, Edith and her sister prepared to take a trip to the Caribbean. The journey may have been some effort at a reconciliation following Edith's rather harsh treatment of Emily during the previous winter. It would also give her a long-overdue vacation from the children and the responsibilities of being First Lady of the state of New York. The two planned to be gone for about a month, beginning on March 7, 1900. The timing of the trip also meant that Edith would exchange the final throes of the New York winter for the tropical heat of Cuba. The two women would be the personal guest of Theodore's old commander, General Leonard Wood, who was now Governor-General of Cuba.

As for the political questions that she was leaving behind, Edith firmly believed that they had been settled. She believed that her husband would run for the governorship and be easily reelected to a second term in office. However, while she was away, various elements within the Republican Party continued to advance Roosevelt's name as a potential vice-presidential candidate. There was an interesting convergence of political foes behind this movement. The reform elements of the Party wanted Roosevelt in order to symbolize the growing progressivism of the Party. Meanwhile, many of the conservative elements of the Republican Party perceived the possibility of getting rid of Roosevelt and his front-page appeal by putting in the relatively obscure position of vice president where he would have little opportunity to influence policy.

Edith and Emily landed in Havana on March 10. To all accounts, the two women had an exceptional time. This was Edith's first experience with the tropics, other than her brief period of time at Tampa in Florida. She developed a lifelong fondness for the region and would ultimately return again and again. Edith was especially happy to be retracing the steps of her husband's actions during the Spanish-American War and she was able to see many of the sites and places that he had mentioned in his letters home during the conflict. She would also later admit that she really enjoyed the balmy atmosphere. The trip also served to repair any emotional distance that had grown between the two sisters.

Upon her return, Edith found that she had to almost immediately deal with questions over the vice-presidency, a matter that she had thought settled. Rumors continued to swirl that Roosevelt would accept the nomination and there was a steady stream of speculation in the press over the future of the young governor of New York. While Edith vehemently opposed any more consideration of the nomination, Theodore seemed to be hedging his bets and endeavoring to keep his options open. Although he disavowed any interest in the vice-presidency, he also refused to publically announce that he would refuse the nomination if it was offered to him.

Chapter 6

NATIONAL POLITICS AND
THE VICE-PRESIDENCY

A s First Lady of the state of New York, Edith had achieved a level of comfort and stability that she was loath to surrender. Especially when giving-up the governor's mansion in Albany meant both a cut in pay and a less visible political position for her husband. However, her husband continued to be far less unyielding about the possibility. In May of 1900, the couple set-off for a visit to Washington. Roosevelt seems to have led Edith to believe that the purpose of the trip was to ensure that the more influential members of the Republican Party understood his opposition to the nomination. In reality, the trip was designed to gauge the sentiment of the political leadership. Complicating matters was the selection of Roosevelt as a state representative to the Republican National Convention. This meant that Roosevelt would be at Philadelphia, the site of the Convention, if there was a movement to draft him as the vice-presidential candidate. Roosevelt could easily have avoided service as a state representative, but the fact that he was going to Philadelphia only fanned the flames of the movement to nominate him to be vice president.

PROLOGUE

Although she must have been aware of the growing pressure for a Roosevelt nomination, Edith prepared to attend the Philadelphia convention with enthusiasm. This would be the first time that she had been to a national political convention and that her husband was going to be one of the stars at Philadelphia was doubtless pleasing to her. When Edith and Theodore arrived in Philadelphia on June 16, 1900, they were immediately mobbed by enthusiastic crowds of supporters. Over the next several days, they could not leave their hotel room without drawing more crowds. In addition, there were signs, placards and campaigns buttons everywhere around the city of brotherly love which championed a Roosevelt vice-presidential nomination.

Edith began to sense that the allure of his supporters and the political pressure from above had combined to weaken Theodore's tepid resolve to not accept the nomination. One major opponent to Roosevelt's nomination was Ohio political boss, Mark Hanna. The conservative Hanna was almost distraught over the potential that Roosevelt might be vice president, especially since the young reformer might use the position as a stepping stone to the presidency in 1904. At one point when speaking to a group of Republican leaders, Hanna was said to have exclaimed "don't any of you realize that there's only one life between this madman and the presidency?"[1] Hanna arranged to meet with Roosevelt in his hotel. He pointed asked Roosevelt for a statement that he would refuse the nomination. Under pressure from Edith, Roosevelt initially consented. Hanna then left to report the good news, from his point of view, to the various state delegations that Roosevelt would decline a nomination.

Surrounded by his inner circle, including Edith and his friend Henry Cabot Lodge, Roosevelt spent the afternoon drafting a message. Edith gave her seal of approval to a very blunt message which plainly presented Roosevelt's refusal to accept a vice-presidential nomination. However, Theodore declared that he wished to work on the draft. By this point, he clearly was interested in the position, and could not bring himself to categorically refuse the post, even with Edith's strong urging.

At 4:00 that afternoon, Roosevelt issued a confusing statement that clearly left the door open for his nomination:

> In view of the revival of the talk of myself as a Vice-Presidential candidate, I have this to say. It is impossible too deeply to express how touched I am by the attitude of those delegates, who have wished me to take the nomination . . . . I understand the high honor and dignity of the office, an office so high and

---

[1] This often quoted line is cited in Margaret Leech, *In the Days of McKinley* (New York: Harper's, 1959), p. 537.

so honorable that it is well worthy of the ambition of any man in the United States. But while appreciating all this to the full, I nevertheless feel most deeply that the field of my best usefulness to the public and to the party is in New York State; and that, if the party should see fit to renominate me for Governor, I can in that position help the National ticket as in no other way. I very earnestly hope and ask that every friend of mine in the Convention respect my wish and my judgement in this matter.[2]

By not saying "no" to the nomination, Roosevelt tacitly lent his approval to the efforts to draft him, and everyone, including Edith, realized this. She understood that he would never again accede to her wishes on political matters, no matter how strenuously she asserted herself.

Roosevelt's nomination was almost theatrical. His friend Senator Lodge had been elected chairman of the convention and it had already been decided that Roosevelt himself would second the official nomination for McKinley to be the Party's nominee for the presidency. On June 20, Roosevelt entered the convention hall. Edith had already been seated in the gallery and Roosevelt waved to her as he approached the stage and the band played Theodore's theme song from his time in Cuba, "There'll be a Hot Time in the Old Town Tonight." The crowd responded with thunderous rounds of applause. Roosevelt's seconding speech brought the delegates to their feet as he proclaimed:

We stand on the threshold of a new century big with the fate of mighty nations. It rests with us now to decide whether in the opening years of that century we shall march forward to fresh triumphs or whether at the outset we shall cripple ourselves for the contest. Is America a weakling, to shrink from the work of the great world powers? No. The young giant of the West stands on a continent and clasps the crest of an ocean in either hand. Our nation, glorious in youth and strength, looks into the future with eager eyes and rejoices as a strong man to run a race . . .[3]

With that speech, Roosevelt's nomination was assured. Ultimately, Roosevelt himself was the only delegate at the convention to vote against his nomination. It was reported that Edith, "with just a little grasp of regret . . .

---

[2] Morrison, p. 1337.

[3] Theodore Roosevelt, *Works*, ed. Herman Hagedorn, 14 (New York: Charles Scribner's Sons, 1926), pp. 342-45.

broke into smiles, as she, once and for all, accepted the situation with a grace worthy of a true patriot."[4]

VICE PRESIDENT ROOSEVELT

In spite of her misgivings, Edith realized that she now had to support Theodore to the fullest. With the combined popularity of McKinley and Roosevelt, the election was essentially assured. Edith may secretly have wished for a defeat, but to the public and the family she played the role of dutiful political wife. While her husband crisscrossed the nation campaigning from July to October, Edith was once again left to oversee the children and begin the preparations to move since win or lose, the Roosevelts would have to leave the governor's mansion. Roosevelt's pace was relentless, by election day, he had campaigned in 24 different states, given 673 speeches and traveled a total distance of 21,209 miles.[5]

During the election of 1900, the Republican Party had its greatest electoral success since the election of Ulysses S. Grant in 1872. After the election, Edith and Theodore worked to prepare for their departure from Albany. The couple spent the remaining weeks of November and all of December transferring items from Albany to Oyster Bay and preparing for the inauguration. In February, Roosevelt departed for a seven-week hunting trip.

Perhaps as a display of her contempt for their new position, Edith only planned to be in Washington for a few days during the inauguration before she returned to Sagamore Hill where she would spend the spring and summer. During this period, there was no official residence for the vice president and his family, so Edith had to find a house to rent. The move to Washington would mark the fourth time that the family had changed residences in a six-year period. While Edith had the intricacies of such a move now down to an exact science, she remained unhappy about the move. She also resented her husband's departure for his hunting expedition in Colorado in the midst of the move.

For once, Roosevelt's escapism may have been forgivable. He was exchanging an office in which he both enjoyed and had considerable success in, for a relatively lackluster position. Roosevelt himself would have little to

---

[4] *World* (22 June 1900); quoted in Morris, p. 205.

[5] Morrison, pp1508-10.

during his tenure as vice president. He would have to preside over the opening and closing of each session of the Senate and be prepared to cast the deciding vote should any vote in the Senate result in a tie. Otherwise, the office had very few duties. To compound matters, now that he was vice president, Roosevelt had to make a conscious effort not to upstage the President. This was particularly hard for the image conscious Roosevelt. Nonetheless, he avoided reporters during his hunting trip and even canceled his plans to attend the Rough Riders Reunion that year.

On March 4, 1901, Theodore and Edith rode behind the McKinley's to the Capitol where the President and Vice President-elect took the oath of office. Edith thought the ceremony itself was pleasant and was impressed by the display of affection that the public had for her husband. One anonymous donor even had a $3,000 floral arrangement sent to Bamie's house where the family stayed during the inauguration–a cost equivalent to the annual rent on the Roosevelt's new rented home in Washington.[6] Following the oath of office, which was conducted in the Senate chambers because of rain, Edith and the children watched the inaugural parade from a third-story room which was specially rented for the occasion. That night Theodore, Edith and Alice attended the Inaugural Ball. Alice had a miserable time because she was not allowed to join the dancing and was "reproved" for sitting on the arm of Mrs. McKinley's chair.[7] Alice was also unhappy because Edith made her wear a dress whose style the daughter saw as too juvenile. Alice asserted that "it was like wearing a label that said, 'This person is very young'."[8] Immediately after the inauguration, at 10:00 the next morning, Edith and the children boarded a train for Oyster Bay.

Roosevelt's official duties lasted four days. He presided over the opening of the Senate and after a few official meetings with the Cabinet, he presided over the close of the Senate for the summer recess on March 8, 1901. The idleness of the new position led Roosevelt to write to his friend Robert Taft, who was Governor-General of the Philippines, that he "had very ugly feelings now and then that I am leading a life of unwarrantable idleness."[9] Matters were made worse by the realization that McKinley had no desire for

---

[6] Morris, p. 207.

[7] Teague, p. 61.

[8] Longworth, p. 37.

[9] Theodore Roosevelt to Robert Taft, April 26, 1901, Morrison.

Roosevelt's advice or counsel. The President seemed determined to prevent Roosevelt from exerting any significant influence over the administration. At one point, Roosevelt even told Edith and many of his friends that he thought the office should be done away with.

Throughout her life, Edith had a tumultuous relationship with her stepdaughter. Despite periods of intense conflict between the two, they often had equally tender moments and were in many ways as close as a mother and daughter could be, especially in light of Edith's reserved nature and Alice's tempestuousness personality. The spring and summer of 1901 marked one of their better periods. After Edith rented the house in Washington, she let Alice choose which children would go in which rooms. In May, Theodore, Edith and Alice traveled north to Buffalo to witness the opening of the Pan-American Exposition. The three had very enjoyable time. For Alice, it was her "first experience of being a grown-up member of an official family" and to all accounts, she behaved very well and did not engage in the kind of antics that had caused problems with her parents in the past.[10] The family "took in all the lighter entertainments" of the Exposition, and Alice even got to see the "hoochee-koochee" dancers.[11] For Edith and Theodore, it was a chance to spend time together without the burden of office or the necessity of caring for the other children. When Alice and her parents returned to Oyster Bay for the remainder of the summer, Edith and her stepdaughter began to plan the latter's social debut.

While the summer passed without significant event, there were the minor crises of family life. Archie contracted the chicken pox. Alice developed an abscess in her jaw from her previous injury. Although the dentist wanted to remove several of her teeth, she resisted and was supported by Edith. Both were strenuously opposed to the idea of Alice appearing at her social debut with false teeth. While Alice was still in the hospital, Quentin joined her because of a major ear infection. During this same period, Theodore managed to come down with bronchitis.

---

[10] Longworth, p. 38.

[11] Ibid., p. 39.

INTO THE FIRE

Theodore had a brief speaking tour planned for the end of the summer and Edith decided to take advantage of his absence and have a short vacation with the children. She rented a cabin in the Adirondacks and departed with the children. Theodore planned to meet the family there during the first week of September. On September 6, while Roosevelt attended a luncheon of the Vermont Fish and Game League, he received a telephone call that President McKinley had been shot in Buffalo by a Polish anarchist named Leon Czolgosz. Roosevelt immediately left for Buffalo. On September 7, Edith and her youngest daughter Ethel visited the campsite of a family friend. On their return, Edith received news of the incident. The assassination attempt shocked her ordered view of the world and reinforced her concerns about her husband's safety. She was significantly relieved after she was able to have a telephone conversation with Theodore the following day. Her husband told her that the wound was not serious and that he would meet them at their cabin on September 12.

The doctors initially believed that McKinley would make a full recovery. The President was in good health before the gunshot wounds, only one of which appeared to be serious. One bullet had penetrated McKinley's stomach and could not be retrieved. However, there did not appear to be any sign of infection and Roosevelt was urged to go to the Adirondacks as a signal to the American people that there was no major crisis and the President was in good health. Ultimately, the wound did grow infected and McKinley's health began to decline rapidly after Roosevelt departed.

The day of his arrival, Roosevelt announced that he intended to scale Mt. Marcy, the highest peak in the area. Edith, Kermit and Ethel accompanied Roosevelt and a small party the conservationist James McNaughton. On the morning of the thirteenth, the party began its ascent. Rain in the morning led Edith to return to the base of the mountain with the children, but Theodore and the rest of the party continued their climb. They reached the summit before noon and were having lunch when a messenger appeared with a telegraph that informed the Vice President that the President's condition had worsened. The party hurriedly descended. Edith heard the news before Theodore and was prepared when her husband arrived at six in the evening. Dinner was prepared for the bone-drenched and weary hikers, but Edith had been unable to find-out any more news. Roosevelt decided to remain at the camp until he received further news. He was hesitant to leave the location where his party was known to be in case future messages were on route. He also did not want to impose himself on the McKinley family during this period of crisis. Finally, after the physical toll of the day's climb, Roosevelt wanted to be rested in case the next few days were as trying as they potentially could be.

He went to bed at nine, but was awakened after eleven with reports that McKinley's condition had worsened and that the President's could die at any time. Roosevelt hurriedly dressed and set off on a wagon with a single driver as his only escort. After a journey of thirty-five miles through twisting mountain roads, the Vice President was met by his official secretary, William Loeb, who informed him that McKinley had died at 2:15 in the morning. Roosevelt sent a message to Edith informing her of what happened and then boarded a specially commandeered train and set off for Buffalo, some 400 miles away.

Edith realized that the family vacation was over and prepared the children for their journey back to Oyster Bay. After breakfast, the family began their journey. When they entered Lower Works, the nearest small village, Edith was given her husband's telegraph informing her of the President's death. By the time the Roosevelt's had completed the first leg of their train ride home, Edith received the news that her husband had taken the oath of office as the twenty-sixth president of the United States.

In Buffalo, Theodore found himself pulled in many directions. He offered his condolences to the grieving Ira McKinley, but members of the Cabinet wanted him to immediately take the Presidential Oath which was delivered by a local judge. There were plans and details of the transition that needed to be resolved, and statements had to be issued to the press. Roosevelt worried about public perceptions of his actions during the crisis and about his ability to conduct or implement the policies he felt the nation needed, and yet remain respectful of the McKinley legacy. He was very conscious that his would be, at least of the remainder of his first term, a "borrowed" presidency.

The impact of the new office on Edith was almost traumatic. She had just barely resigned herself to being the wife of the Vice President. Edith realized that the office of First Lady was going to require adjustments that she had hoped she would never have to make. There would be the inevitable loss of privacy that life in the White House and her duties as first lady would entail. In addition, she was concerned over both the safety and privacy of her children and, in light of recent events, especially the safety of her husband.

There were also a variety of both major and minor tasks that required her immediate attention. Despite the looming responsibilities on the horizon, Edith was first and foremost a mother. On the return trip to Oyster Bay, Quentin managed to get a small stone lodged in his ear and Edith was forced to stop the trip and find a doctor to remove it.

Chapter 7

THE WHITE HOUSE YEARS

Edith Roosevelt's official debut as First Lady occurred on September 16, 1901 when she met her husband in Washington as he escorted McKinley's body back to the capitol for the official ceremony to mark his passage. From the beginning, Edith had a very positive relationship with the national press. This was the result of a combination of factors. To begin with, Edith's personality was well suited for her office at the time. She possessed the right mixture of self-assurance and simplicity to make her attractive to the American people. In public, she always appeared calmed and self-assured. Her quiet nature reinforced this image. In addition, years of economizing and working diligently to maintain the family's finances had grounded her tastes. This ensured that although she was very conscious of the importance of style and image, Edith was also very attuned to the financial ramifications of ostentatiousness. She was well suited to takeover the fiscal responsibilities of First Lady and management of the Executive Mansion.

Her first public relations coup occurred as she traveled to meet her husband. On the train ride from New York to Washington, Edith journeyed without a maid. The contemporary press praised this as an example of "her simple habits and democratic tastes."[1] Such stories resonated with the American public at a time when the backlash against the "glittering age" of the 1890s and the robber barrens of industry and commerce, including such figures as J.P. Morgan, was nearing its height. In spite of their wealthy and socially prominent backgrounds, Edith and Theodore were seen as

---

[1]. *World* (September 17, 1901); quoted in Morris, p. 219.

representative of the common values and ethics of the average American. During her time as First Lady, Edith paid little attention to her hair and more significantly, she refused to wear foreign gowns. Instead she used American designers and American clothes.[2]

At the time, the President's salary was $50,000 per year. This was the largest salary that Theodore had ever made. In addition, the President's expenses were generously reimbursed and Edith also had discretion over household spending and money for the staff. Nonetheless, she maintained her frugal habits. Even when she purchased new furniture or wall dressings for the White House, Edith would not throw the old items away, but simply use them elsewhere in the mansion. She always had an eye for the future and wanted to make sure that when Theodore's tenure as President was over, that the family would be financially secure.

When Edith first arrived in Washington, she and Theodore continued to reside at their rented home which became in effect a second Executive Mansion. This delay in moving into the president's official residence was occasioned by the desire to let Ira McKinley remain in the White House until she had regained her composure. After the ceremonies to mark McKinley's death were complete, Roosevelt accompanied the body to Canton, Ohio, where the former president was buried. Meanwhile Edith returned to Sagamore Hill to prepare the children for the move to Washington. Ira McKinley's few weeks at the White House would allow Edith to prepare for the transition. Meanwhile, time at Oyster Bay would also grant her a period of rest and recovery before she was plunged into the intricacies of life as first lady.

Theodore moved into the Executive Mansion on September 23 and Edith followed him two days later. The family would place an indelible stamp on the president's home and were the source of many of the traditions and customs associated with the Executive Mansion. For instance, Theodore renamed the Executive Mansion the "White House." The Roosevelts were the largest family with young child ever to occupy the White House. The family was also one of the most energetic and lively groups to live there. After overcoming any initial awe of the mansion, the youngest children often engaged in pranks and other childhood acts, none of which were seriously

---

[2] Carl Anthony Sferrazza Anthony, *America's First Families: An Inside View of 200 Years of Private Life in the White House* (New York: Touchstone, 2000), pp. 332-34.

harmful, but many of which were embarrassing to Edith and Theodore. The Roosevelts also had to contend with Alice who grew increasingly mischievous in her late teens. In addition, the Roosevelt zoo only grew during the family's residency in the White House as Theodore's fondness for animals led foreign dignitaries and officials to give him various exotic animals as pets. Through it all, Edith managed to maintain the image of the family that corresponded with the office, even if it did not always correspond to reality.

REMAKING THE WHITE HOUSE

Edith was significantly disappointed when she first accessed the White House. The private living spaces were too small to accommodate the family. The first floor of the mansion was devoted to office space and rooms for official functions and even the second floor had offices. The private living space of the first family consisted of five bedrooms, a guestroom, a reception hall and a library. Edith and Theodore were both used to having a private office to work from and while Theodore's working space would be more than adequate because of his use of the official offices, Edith wished a place of her own where she could remove herself from the cares and concerns of her station and family. She also realized that the children and the inevitable family members and guests who would visit the White House would need more room.

Besides the small personal quarters, Edith was profoundly struck by a sense of gloom and darkness in the family's new home. Alice would describe the interior of the mansion as "both ugly and inconvenient."[3] In a "symbolic" act, Edith ordered the windows opened so as to air-out the mansion and allow in sunlight.[4] The new First Lady also arranged for fresh flowers to be brought in on a regular basis in order to improve the air and look of the mansion. She then began rearranging the White House. As she had done with the governor's mansion in New York, Edith set out to make this official residence a real home for the family. Functional furniture was brought in, as were new books and paintings. For instance, Edith removed the antique beds in the bedrooms of her sons and replaced them with modern and almost indestructible cast-iron bedframes in order to prevent damage to the nation's artifacts. Edith made the

---

[3] Longworth, p. 44.
[4] Morris, p. 223.

large suite in the southwest corner of the White House the presidential bedroom and she and Theodore slept in the Lincoln bed. She had the bedroom suite which was formerly known as the "Queen's Suite" in honor of the several European monarchs who had stayed there, turned into a guest apartment for family members. Her sister Emily and various members of the Roosevelt clan would ultimately use the facility which Edith also renamed as the Rose Suite. She confiscated the upstairs library and made it into her private office. The room was connected to her husband's own office so that as they had done at Oyster Bay, the two could communicate while Theodore was working and while Edith oversaw the family's correspondence and accounts. This arrangement also afforded Edith the ability to make sure that Theodore did not get carried away in his work since she could get him when he invariably stayed up too late or became absorbed in some project and forgot other commitments. Edith also began a broad campaign to have the White House renovated.

Even before the Roosevelts entered the White House, there had been multiple proposals to renovate the Executive Mansion. Presidents including Benjamin Harrison and William McKinley proposed design changes and modernization programs. Edith and Theodore decided to advance a renovation that would both expand the mansion to allow for more personal areas and restore the building to its original decor by stripping many of the architectural additions that had been added through the years. Roosevelt approached an old friend, Charles McKim, who happened to be one of the nation's foremost architects at the time about preparing plans for the changes. Edith had a significant influence on the design of the family quarters and met several times with the architect. McKim's design won immediate approval from the Roosevelts and it so impressed Congress that it voted to begin construction the following year. In total, Congress appropriated $541,361 for the project. Of this amount, just over $475,000 would be spend on the renovation while the remaining funds were appropriated for the construction of a "West Wing" of offices. In order to complete the project, several areas of the floor of the first level of the White House had to be reinforced and glass green houses on the lawn had to be removed in order to build the West Wing. When the work was completed, the family spaces had been vastly enlarged and many offices were moved to the West Wing. Other specific areas, including the State Dining Room, were also expanded. In addition, the White House had new plumbing, heating and electrical systems and even an elevator, all of which were put in place to bring the building into the twentieth-century. Furthermore, the interior of the building had been refurbished so that its decor was more uniform and modern. Many of the quirky or mismatched accessories were removed. For instance Edith had "the velvety, fringed, potted palm look of the East Room . . . replaced by elegant yellow and gold."[5]

Indeed, it was in the redecoration of the interior spaces that Edith had the most influence. In addition to choosing new fixtures and accouterments, Edith selected new china and silverware. She also initiated the White House China Collection and began the portrait gallery of the First Ladies. In order to ensure that her efforts would be long-lasting and that future residents of the mansion would be hesitant to remove articles for souvenirs, Edith was established the first comprehensive inventory of household items, including china and flatware, furniture, linens and wall hangings.[6] By ensuring that the renovations were consistent with the original style of the Executive Mansion, Edith "set the precedent for thinking of the White House as a museum of U.S. history and the presidency."[7]

The First Lady also exercised a considerable amount of influence over the exterior grounds. With the greenhouses removed to make way for the West Wing, Edith established a "Colonial garden" to replace them.[8] This garden usually contained various multi-colored bulbs and perennials. Edith also sought to maintain the lawn of the White House. Her efforts to do so led her to oppose the annual Easter egg-rolling contests on the South Lawn. This event had its official origins with the Hayes administration, and had grown in popularity since then. In spite of Edith's disapproval, egg rolling was very popular with Theodore and the children.

During the six-month period of construction, Roosevelt moved to a temporary address, while Edith and the children stayed at Sagamore Hill. Theodore joined them at Oyster Bay during the summer. On September 3, 1902, Roosevelt was involved in a trolley accident which produced what seemed to be only a minor injury to his leg. However, by September 23, doctors had to operate on his leg. Although it was not debilitating, the injury bothered him for the rest of his life. When she learned about the operation,

---

[5] Betty Boyd Caroli, *The Roosevelt Women* (New York: Basic Book, 1998), p. 198.

[6] Morris, p. 254.

[7] Robert P. Watson, *The President's Wives: Reassessing the Office of First Lady* (Boulder: Lynne Reinner, 2000), p. 80.

[8] Sferrazza, p. 63.

Edith hurried back to Washington to be at her husband's side. Roosevelt recovered sufficiently to be ready for the reopening of the White House in October. The family officially moved back in on November 5.

FAMILY LIFE

Throughout their stay in the White House, the daily routine of the First Family varied little. She divided her day into family hours and official "office hours." Edith had long ago realized the importance of consistency for the children, especially in light of their otherwise rambunctious behaviors. Each morning, the family would have breakfast at about quarter-after eight. During the meal, the quiet Edith encouraged the children to talk about their days and activities. This pattern reinforced the closeness of the children with their parents. Alice would recall that the most unfortunate part of these breakfasts was having to kiss Theodore who inevitably still had shaving cream in his mustache. Following breakfast, Edith and Theodore would often go for a walk around the grounds. Returning by about 9:30 or 9:45, Edith would begin her oversight of the household management, while her husband commenced his official duties. Edith would look through her correspondence, writing the necessary replies and thank you notes, reading the leading newspapers and preparing any paperwork, such as guest lists, which needed her attention.

Unlike her predecessors, Edith did not use an official housekeeper to oversee the staff and manage the household. She preferred to handle these tasks herself. Before lunch, Edith usually conducted any meetings that were necessary. This might include conferences with the cooks over upcoming state dinners or meetings with various governmental officials. She and Theodore regularly had lunch at about 1:00 o'clock in the afternoon. Lunch was usually an adventure since Edith seldom knew in advance who was going to be there. Theodore developed the habit of bringing to lunch whatever officials or guests he was meeting with at the appointed hour. This often led to a strange cast at lunch and provoked some fascinating conversations that would later be recalled by participants. Roosevelt added to the bohemian flavor by mixing "discussions of birds, brief and incisive analyses of political questions, unexpected quotations from Kipling and Swinburne, descriptions of throws he had just learned from his Japanese wrestling instructors, recollections of his

Rough Rider days, and sudden references to Euripides or the lore of the Nibelungenlied."[9]

After lunch, Edith reserved time to conduct meetings and then would go riding in the afternoon. She was an excellent horsewomen and sincerely enjoyed riding. Edith also recognized the health benefits of exercise and through her regular afternoon rides may have been the first First Lady to habitually exercise. Just before dinner, Edith read to the children, and often as not, she was joined by Theodore. After dinner, she often read to family again.

Reading was a favorite pastime of the family. From birth, Edith and Theodore constantly read to the children. As they grew, each of the children became voracious readers. Ike Hoover, who spent 48 years serving various First Families, characterized the entire family as

> fiends when it came to reading . . . . Never a moment was allowed to go to waste. From the eldest to the youngest they always had a book or magazine before them. The President in particular would just devour a book, and it was no uncommon thing for him to go through three or four volumes in the course of an evening. Likewise we frequently saw one of the children stretched out on the floor flat on his stomach eating a piece of candy and with his face buried deep in a book.[10]

In this fashion, the children became acquainted with both the major literary works of the day and popular fiction. The children read the works of Rudyard Kipling, one of Theodore's favorite authors and poets, Walter Scott and Charles Dickens, as well as classic pieces by Shakespeare. More significantly, the family routinely discussed the works that they had read and the children were expected to join in the literary debates.

When the Roosevelts moved into the White House, the eldest son, Ted, had already began his education at Groton, considered to be the most exclusive preparatory school in the United States. Kermit, Archie, and eventually, Quentin, went to public schools until they were old enough to attend Groton. At school, the Roosevelt boys were treated the same as other pupils. This greatly impressed the press and public. Soon stories and pictures of the President's children sitting side-by-side with other pupils were common and reinforced the egalitarian perception of the First Family. This common

---

[9] Kathleen Prindiville, *First Ladies* (New York: MacMillan, 1932), p. 200.
[10] Kerr, p. 55.

belief was given further credence by the very active role that Edith and Theodore took in their children's education. It was not uncommon for a teacher to receive notes from the President or First Lady. When Quentin hit a teacher in the back of the head with a spitball, the entire school was shocked the following morning when they received a visit from the President of the United States bearing a bouquet of flowers for the teacher and an official apology.

While Ethel was enrolled at the Cathedral School, Alice evaded being enrolled in school by employing the same tactics that she had used when Roosevelt was governor. She had an almost photographic memory and in spite of her lack of formal education, was one of the most well-read and literate young women of Washington society. When the boys reached the appropriate age, they followed Ted to Groton. All did well, with the exception of Archie who was expelled after writing some minor disparaging comments about the school to friend (and having the note confiscated by school officials). Archie would finish his education at the prestigious boys school, Andover.

In addition to raising the children, Edith found that she also had to take care of her other child, Theodore. In many ways, her husband behaved as rambunctiously as the children. Just before they were packed off to bed, Theodore usually played "bear" with the children. These wrestling matches were favorite times for the children and the President. On more than one occasion, Roosevelt was late to official functions because he was playing with the children or because his clothes became ruffled and had to be changed before he made his appearance.

Despite the close almost fraternal relationship that Theodore had with his children, it was he, not Edith, who meted-out discipline to the children. Even before the birth of her younger children, Edith developed a habit of simply ignoring all but the most egregious actions of the children. She seemed ready and willing to accept the minor pranks and shenanigans of her sons and daughters as being some manifestation of the Roosevelt genes. While Theodore was generally in charge of punishing the children, the only time he acknowledged physically "thrashing" one of children was when Quentin came home from school without permission from the school and lied to his parents about the episode.

An outgrowth of Roosevelt's boyish nature was the development of the Roosevelt "zoo." Roosevelt enjoyed animals and, as aforementioned, he believed in their intrinsic value to the children. As a consequence, the

Roosevelt family zoo grew steadily while Theodore was president. There was already a long list of family dogs and several ponies. Furthermore, new dogs would be added. When Edith's favorite house dog "Tip" died, she immediately went to the Washington dog pound and chose another–and thereby added to the public perception of her democratic and egalitarian nature. When the family entered the White House, guinea pigs were the favorite pets of the boys, especially since they were small enough to be smuggled around inside their jackets. Roosevelt's penchant for animals led many foreign dignitaries and heads of state to give various exotic animals to the President. In one year alone, Roosevelt received a lion, zebra, hyena, five bears, and numerous birds, snakes and lizards. Many of the more exotic animals were given to the Washington Zoo, but Roosevelt kept one bear and the children retained a variety of strange pets, including a badger, several kangaroo rats and assorted flying squirrels.

One major change that affected the family after they moved into the White House, was the increased level of security. Edith, who was a very private person, was unaccustomed to the presence of the secret service even though during this period the numbers of agents assigned to the President and First Family was minimal compared with the staff of today. Even though their presence was somewhat unsettling to Edith, in light of the manner in which her husband became President, she greatly appreciated the need for security. Concerns over her husband's safety would often cloud Edith's enjoyment of the White House. It would be Edith who arranged for extra security for the family at Oyster Bay and at the Virginia getaway, Pine Knot, that Roosevelt purchased while President. In later life, she would cite this fear as one of the reasons she was happy to see Theodore retire from politics.

Although she had been a political wife for over a decade, Edith never had experienced the kind of public scrutiny that being First Lady brought upon her and the family. She was especially worried that the press would present the family in an unfavorable light. This was especially true because of what she considered to be the quirks of the family. These eccentricities included the boys' general behavior and their pranks, as well as Alice's increasingly defiant behavior. Off all of the children, Alice was the one that truly enjoyed the public eye. Following her 1902 debut in Washington, she became one of the social icons of Washington. At the party, Corrine noted that Alice had "men

seven deep around her all the time."[11] The debut was the social event of the
year and helped revive the White House as the social center of Washington. In
Edith's eyes, Alice's greatest affront to the family was her smoking. Despite
the intervention of both Edith and Theodore, Alice would not stop the habit.

In order to control or at least manage the public's conception of the
family, Edith employed a variety of tactics. First, she tried to prevent the
children from talking to the press. While this edict worked with the younger
children, Alice would grow increasingly vocal and flamboyant as she grew-up
in the White House. Second, in the days before television and radio, she
carefully oversaw the dissemination of information to the press. She and
members of her staff would often rewrite stories of social events or
happenings at the White House so as to craft a carefully constructed vision of
the family. Edith frequently had staged photographs taken of the family on the
White House lawn. These pictures seemed to present a view of the family as
sedate and scholarly. Edith even hired a personal photographer, Francis
Benjamin Johnson, so she could ensure control over the pictures. For his part,
Johnson did a masterful job of taking pictures which conveyed a deep sense of
intimacy on the part of the family. Third, and finally, Edith carefully chose the
events that the family attended. She tried to avoid events where she would not
be able to control the children, especially if there was going to be a large press
presence. Edith would also meticulously plan the social events at the White
House. Instead of being directly involved in the preparation of food or the
setting of the event, Edith allowed caterers and the staff take care of details,
while she concentrated on the planning and design of the White House
functions.

Edith's aggressive approach to managing the press contrasted sharply with
her two predecessors. Frances Cleveland had tried to maintain her privacy and
had shunned contact with the media. Concurrently, Ida McKinley's infirmities
had prevented her from appearing in public. Edith's management of the press
still meant that there was a significant increase in the number of photographs
and stories about her and the First Family. Edith's photograph even graced the
cover of *Ladies' Home Journal*.[12] When combined with the perception of her
as a symbol of democracy and egalitarianism, Edith's visible presence in the
press reinforced her public popularity.

---

[11] Ibid., p. 69.

[12] Margaret Truman, *First Ladies* (New York: Random House, 1996), p. 307.

THE OFFICIAL FIRST LADY

Just as she was essentially the first First Lady of the twentieth century in chronological terms, Edith was also the first modern First Lady and brought to the position many of the innovations and elements of style that would come to characterize the office. Her predecessor Ira McKinley had been unable to perform many of the duties of office because of her health. Consequently, just as she had seemed to breath life again into the White House, she also seemed to revive the office of First Lady to the American public. As with so much of the rest of her life, Edith worked to carefully craft her image and to manage all aspects of her official duties in great specificity.

One of her first decisions was to hire Isabelle "Belle" Hagner as her social secretary. With this action, Edith became the first First Lady to have an official social assistant. Hagner's pay was $1,400 per year, and her duties ranged from helping Edith with correspondence to arranging guest lists to dealing with the press. In fact, the First Lady often used Hagner as an intermediary with the press. Edith and Belle would draft stories of about the activities of the children or the family and the secretary would then disseminate these narratives to the Washington press corps. Hagner also helped Edith oversee the social events at the White House. Edith quickly came to rely on the managerial and administrative talents of Hagner. Family friend Archie Butt described being "astonished" at Hagner's executive abilities and claimed that "she really is the chief factor at the White House."[13] The woman's abilities would lead other first ladies to employ her, including Edith Wilson.

With Hagner handling many of the routine and often dull aspects of protocol and dealing with the press, Edith had more time to devote toward the children and to running the household (a role that she clearly felt more comfortable in). Hence, while Hagner met with members of the press, Edith would often be meeting with the household staff. Hagner's competence also allowed Edith more free time so that she could occasionally go shopping or antiquing in and around Washington. Her secretary handled Edith's schedule book, and it was said that even Corrine and Bamie needed appointments if they wanted to see the First Lady.

---

[13] Butt, p. 53.

One of Edith's main concerns as First Lady was to ensure the preeminence of the White House as the social center of Washington. Although Theodore was making more money than he ever had, Edith understood that even with her husband as President, it would be difficult to match the parties and balls of some of Washington's wealthier families. Therefore, she endeavored to concentrate on style and publicity, rather than trying to compete with the extravagance and splendor of others. The social debut of Alice in 1902 and her later wedding turned out to be among the most prominent social events of the capital and were reported extensively throughout the nation. Edith also ensured that diplomatic receptions and other official functions received the same level of publicity.

In order to actually conduct the events, Edith took what was considered to be the unusual step of having events catered instead of using the White House staff to prepare the meals and serve the guests. On average, the catered events cost the government $8.00 per person, but during the more formal state dinners, the cost rose to $10.00 per person. However, by utilizing a caterer, Edith could concentrate her time on planning the event and then participating in the festivities instead of worrying about the intricacies of serving the meals and the quality of the food and service. It also removed a degree of the burden of the events from the White House staff. Therefore, the Roosevelts were able to have more official functions than otherwise might have been the case since the staff could attend to their regular duties without significant interruptions.

As she planned for social occasions, Edith utilized a sort of master list that she and Belle had put together. The list divided the extended family and society elites, Washington diplomatic corps and members of the government into categories. There was a political group which included society members and governmental dignitaries which had to be included in official or state occasions. There was an inner set which included some members of government such as Cabot Lodge and Elihu Root, but was mainly composed of the Roosevelts' friends and family members. The inner set formed the core of those invited to private family celebrations such as birthdays. Finally, there was Edith's own small circle of friends with whom she would lunch or attend functions. This group included the historian Henry Adams and Theodore's sisters, among others.[14] With this formal categorization, there were never any mistakes and arrangements could be quickly made for any function.

---

[14] Prindiville, pp. 198-99.

Among the wives of the officialdom of Washington, Edith saw herself as a kind of first among equals. She endeavored to create a kind of inner sanctum that included herself and the wives of the senior cabinet officers. Edith met the wives of the cabinet secretaries each Tuesday, while their husbands met with the President. The ladies would discuss the politics of the day, as well as fashion and literature. Besides the since of comradery that these meetings engendered, they also served a very useful political purpose. Edith was able to hear any of the political or social gossip making the rounds of Washington and could therefore pass information on to Theodore. In this informal setting, Edith also had the opportunity to gauge public perceptions of herself and the family–a matter that often preoccupied her attention while she occupied the White House.

Edith's connections with various society figures would lead her to be utilized by Theodore in some diplomatic maneuvers. For instance, in 1905, Roosevelt and the British Ambassador, Sir Mortimer Durand, were in the midst of a minor feud and there was little communication between the two. Instead, Edith would meet with the Roosevelt family friend, Cecil Spring-Rice. Spring-Rice relayed information to Edith on the Russo-Japanese war, and the two bypassed both the British Embassy and the American State Department. This system proved valuable in Roosevelt's decision to mediate the conflict between the two powers. The result of the President's mediation was the Treaty of Portsmouth which ended the war in 1905. For his part in the negotiations that ended the war, Roosevelt became the first American to receive the Nobel Peace Prize on December 10, 1906. The Peace Prize carried with it a $40,000 cash award. After discussing the matter with Edith, Roosevelt decided to donate the money to an effort to establish an international industrial committee which would work to settle disputes between workers and employers.

As First Lady, Edith supported a variety of charitable activities. Some activities were sponsored in an official fashion, while others received their patronage anonymously. Often Edith took an interest in a specific family or charitable case. She researched particular cases and then essentially adopted individuals and families and worked to provide food, shelter and often employment. When people from around the nation wrote letters describing their hard times or problems, Edith often responded after investigating their circumstances. It was not uncommon for people to receive a surprise donation from the White House. Specific examples include Edith's intercession on the behalf of a woman in Missouri who was about to be evicted but instead received funds while arrangements were made to get her husband a job or families who found that their medical bills were paid by the White House. One of Edith's favorite charitable activities was to provide money to the doctors at hospitals that treated the poor. The physicians then dispersed the money to the indigent. At a public level, Edith arranged for baskets and donations of food to be given out to needy families in the nations's capital and other large cities–usually paying for the costs of the donations from her own accounts. Among her favorite formal charities were the Washington Children's Hospital and the Hope and Health Mission. She also liked to help Roosevelt's Rough Rider companions with funds or other aid. Edith saw this as a way to repay her husband's comrades for their support both during the Spanish-American War and during his political career.[15]

During the final two years of his presidency, Roosevelt grew increasingly more supportive of progressive legislation and causes. For instance, in 1907, he asserted that all American corporations should be under the oversight of federal commerce regulations (a radical notion at the time which caused a financial panic). The following year, Roosevelt proposed a worker's compensation plan and federal oversight of railroads and the stock market. Edith supported the proposed reforms and actually lobbied behind the scenes for their passage.

The Roosevelts were generally full of energy and that vigor could not be contained within the walls of the White House. All members of the family traveled extensively, and Theodore became the first sitting President to travel outside of the United States while in office. Meanwhile, Edith became the first presidential spouse to travel extensively, and the most traveled First Lady until her niece Eleanor occupied the White House thirty-some years later.

During the spring of 1903, the family went in separate directions. There was nothing new to this pattern, and it would be repeated on many occasions while the Roosevelts were the First Family. Theodore began a cross-country tour which included meetings with state Republican leaders and stump speeches for the Party's candidates in the fall congressional elections. Meanwhile, in an interesting turn of events, Alice was dispatched on a goodwill tour of first Cuba, and then a year later, Puerto Rico. Just after her social debut, Alice had been invited to christen the new yacht of Kaiser

---

[15] Morris, p. 332.

Wilhelm of Germany, *The Meteor*. Her carriage and demeanor at the ceremony led the press to dub her "Princess Alice." After her success at the event, where she was very well-received by the press, Edith and Theodore decided to send her to England to represent the family at the coronation of King Edward. However diplomatic complications ensued and it was decided that Alice should not go.[16] Instead she would go to the tropics, which Edith, recalling her own experiences, knew Alice would enjoy. After Cuba Alice was dispatched to Puerto Rico in 1903 and then went on an extended tour of the Far East which lasted four months in 1905. During this journey, Alice visited Japan, China, the Philippines, Hong Kong and Korea.

Meanwhile, in that spring of 1903, Edith took the three youngest children on an extended cruise. This would be followed in 1905 with a cruise through the St. John's River in Florida. The culmination of her travels as First Lady would be her journey with Theodore to Panama. This made the Roosevelts the first President and First Lady to travel outside of the United States while in office. Roosevelt's support of Panamanian independence had resulted in a treaty between the two nations to allow the United States to construct a canal across the isthmus. The two set sail on November 8, 1906 and arrived in Panama six days later. The inspected the ongoing construction of the Canal and traveled across the isthmus.

The desire to get away from Washington also manifested itself in Edith's decision in 1905 to purchase a country getaway cabin in the Blue Ridge Mountains of Virginia. Pine Knot was located in Albermarle County, 125 miles from the capital. For Edith, the country house was near enough to allow to escape the pressures and complications of Washington, while Theodore liked the fact that Pine Knot was located in the woods.

FAMILY STRAINS

Alice attracted considerable attention and speculation over her future and potential husband. Her debut had been a resounding success and she quickly begun to draw interest from the opposite sex. Ultimately, a new Republican Congressman from Ohio, Nicholas Longworth, caught Alice's eye. Although "Nick" was fifteen years older than Alice, the two began seeing each other.

---

[16] For Alice's recollections of the event, see Longworth, p. 50.

Upon her return from the Far East in 1905, the engagement of the two was announced with a wedding planned for February, 1906.

The engagement proved to be a trying time for Edith. On one level, Edith believed that Alice was ready to be married. Conscious of her own past, Edith was worried that Alice might become a spinster. She also hoped that marriage might settle Alice down and mature her. At the time of the wedding announcement, Alice was twenty-one years old and Edith was concerned that Alice's reputation might dissuade potential suitors. In addition, the planning for the wedding would significantly tax Edith's capabilities. Edith would have to manage the heavy social season of the presidential mansion and make the arrangements for the wedding which would be held at the White House. Alice proved to be of little help to her stepmother in preparing for the wedding. In the background of the wedding was Edith's disapproval of Nick as a match for Alice. Theodore greatly approved of Nick, but Edith had always been a shrewd judge of character and recognized several problems with Alice's future husband. The Longworth family had a history of alcoholism and alone among the Roosevelts Edith recognized the warning signs in Nick. Furthermore, Longworth had a reputation as a womanizer and his engagement to Alice did not appear to change his habits.

Nonetheless, Edith proceeded with the arrangements of the wedding which took place on February 17, 1906. To the very end Alice proved to be difficult and delayed the wedding ceremony for some time. In the end, the strain produced an uncharacteristic outburst on the part of Edith. After the ceremony, when Alice went to thank Edith for her help during the wedding, Edith snapped loudly enough for all to hear, "I want you to know that I'm glad to see you leave. You have never been anything but trouble."[17] Although Edith and Alice would reconcile, their relationship would remain strained throughout Edith's life. Alice's relationship with her father also remained tense and Alice often felt isolated from the rest of her family. While Ethel and the boys could turn to Edith or Theodore, Alice found herself separated emotionally from her parents and siblings.

Edith's maternal problems did not completely revolve around Alice. By 1904, Quentin was old enough to cause his mother an inordinate amount of embarrassment and vexation. All of the Roosevelt children had been mischievous at the very least, but Quentin's antics rose to an entirely new

---

[17] Caroli, *Roosevelt Women*, p. 405.

level which was complicated by the fact that he was an inhabitant of the White House. His shenanigans included covering the portrait of Andrew Jackson with spitballs and bringing the family pony, Algonquin, into the upstairs of the White House in order to cheer his brother Archie who had the measles at the time.[18]

Tensions between Edith and Theodore's sisters reached their peak while he was president. Ever since Edith advised her husband not to run for mayor of New York, Theodore had relied more on his sisters for political advice and counsel than on his wife. His sisters were also often more active in support of Theodore's political career. Both had been important to him while he was governor and he had used his sisters in various ways to enhance his political career. Both Bamie and Corrine's houses had served as bases for Roosevelt's political meetings as governor. When he became president, this pattern continued.

Edith disliked many of the aspects of political life. She was far more comfortable discussing literature and poetry than she was engaging in political discourse and usually shied away from public dialogues of the politics of the day. She also particularly disapproved of political campaigning. Edith did not like the constant public appearances and the pace of travel. She further did not enjoy the personal contact. In both official ceremonies and in public, Edith avoided touching people. As was her habit, Edith continued to hold flowers in her hands so as not to have to shake hands. The aspect of campaigning which bothered Edith the most the potential for political violence. As her husband became engaged in evermore controversial political battles, including mediating a major coal strike in 1902 and endeavoring to break-up commercial monopolies, Edith genuinely feared for the safety of Theodore and the rest of the family. This concern was particularly acute when Theodore was campaigning and therefore most vulnerable because of his exposure.

Bamie and Corrine shared few of Edith's concerns and enjoyed Theodore's political maneuvers. Their enthusiasm drew Theodore to them for political advice and counsel. Theodore and one or both of his sisters and various friends would often stay-up late into the night talking politics. As often as not, Edith would retire early while the others continued their debates. During one of these marathon sessions in November of 1904, Theodore and Corrine remained up until seven in the morning discussing a range of topics

---

[18] Truman, pp. 311-12.

that extended from American history to Irish politics. Edith went to bed at midnight. Corrine would later attribute Edith's unwillingness to participate in these discussions to the fact that "she was not born a Roosevelt."

Both Bamie and Corrine accompanied Theodore and Edith to the 1900 Republican Party National Convention where he was nominated. Bamie who had a house on N Street in Washington was a frequent visitor to the White House, as was Corrine when she was in the capital. Both sisters and their families attended dinner with the First Family on the initial night that the Roosevelt's moved into the White House and where on the list of guests to be invited to all social events. The extended Roosevelt clan spent both Thanksgivings and Christmases at the White House until Theodore and Edith bought property in Virginia where they began to spend their holidays in a more sedate fashion.

A telling example of Corrine's support for Theodore centered around one of her brother's first political actions. In 1901, Roosevelt invited the noted African-American Booker T. Washington to dine at the White House. Washington was the first African-American to be recognized in such a visible manner since the 1870s. However, there was a public backlash against Roosevelt for his actions. Many leading newspapers and political commentators, especially in the South, condemned the President's gesture. In an obvious show of support, Corrine supplemented her brother's action with a similar invitation for Washington to dine at her New York home.

When Corrine was in the nation's capital, she and Theodore often went for rides during which they discussed politics, literature and the news of the day. On election day in 1904, Roosevelt and Corrine traveled together from Newark to Philadelphia in his private dining car. During the trip, which Corrine later recounted in a book about her brother, Roosevelt expressed his anxiety over the election. He desperately wanted to be elected President in his own right and demonstrate his ability to be elected on his own. Yet he also expressed the importance of his family. After he arrived at the White House that day, he wrote a letter to Corrine he stated that

> As I mounted the White House steps, Edith came to meet me at the door, and I suddenly realized that, after all, no matter what the outcome of the election should prove to be, my *happiness* (Roosevelt's italics) was assured, even though my ambition to have the seal of approval put upon my administration

might not be gratified, for my life with Edith and my children constitutes my *happiness* (Roosevelt's italics). [19]

In spite of Roosevelt's expressions of love for his family, his relationship with his sisters bothered Edith who continued to be jealous of the fact that Theodore turned to them for political advice and not her. In 1980, a survey by *Good Housekeeping* rated Edith as having essentially no political influence on her husband, while first ladies such as Bess Truman and Florence Harding ranked highly.[20]

Edith demonstrated her capacity for retribution toward Theodore's sisters on more than one occasion. While Edith was perceived by the public as quiet and self-reserved, she had a biting wit and could be vengeful at times. One of her children once quipped that "mother never took any prisoners." Edith was an astute enough political wife to only offer her more biting comments to her closest confidants. But within her inner circle, Edith was often described as ruthless toward others. One act on Edith's part created an enormous degree of ill will on Corrine's part. Theodore wanted his 1905 inauguration celebration to be an affair that included the extended Roosevelt clan.

Somehow in the build-up to the event Edith failed to provide enough inaugural tickets for Corrine's children to attend all of the events. Corrine took the misunderstanding to be a sign of Edith's vindictiveness and pettiness. Understanding well Edith's eye for detail and her usually meticulous planning, Corrine felt that the episode could have only been deliberately planned. Adding to this feeling was the inability or unwillingness of Edith to rectify the situation by obtaining more tickets.[21] For her part, Edith was deeply involved in an enormous amount of planning and the period leading up to the inauguration was extremely trying for her. Corrine eventually forgave Edith and even praised her handling of the ceremonies, but there remained an underlying stream of tension between the two former "best" friends for the remainder of their lives.

---

[19] Robinson, p. 218.

[20] Cited in Watson, p. 182.

[21] Caroli, *Roosevelt Women*, p. 184.

Chapter 8

THE EYE OF THE STORM

During 1908, Edith began to prepare for the transition from the White House. Theodore had already proclaimed that he would not run for another term although he was not legally prevented from doing so. Instead, Roosevelt pledged his agreement with George Washington's sage advice that two terms was enough for any person to serve as president because additional time in office could lead to tyranny. Edith and Theodore began to plan for retirement. Theodore would only be 49 years-old and Edith 46, when the family left the White House. Realizing that his presence would be a hindrance to his successor, Roosevelt sought to find a way to gracefully absent himself from the political and public stage.

For her part, Edith also wished for a return to a more quiet life. Her own popularity rivaled that of her husband. To the public, Edith was a symbol of traditional values and the perfect political wife. In her book on the first ladies, Margaret Truman wrote that "Edith Roosevelt left the White House in 1909 arguably the most esteemed, beloved First Lady since Martha Washington."[1].

With Alice married and her other children approaching adulthood and Theodore's political career coming to a close, Edith envisioned a period of peace and relaxation out of the public eye. She would no longer have to worry about Theodore's safety and hopefully, the media and public would lose interest in the family. Meanwhile, the accumulation of Theodore's pay, combined with prudent investments, had provided financial stability. In addition, Roosevelt had already been approached by a number of publishing

---

[1] Truman, p. 313

offices to write his memoirs and a variety of essays, books and articles. He eventually agreed to become the editor of a weekly journal, *The Outlook*, which paid $12,000 per year. This potential stream of income would ensure that the Roosevelt family was able to have a comfortable and prosperous future. This was especially significant since there was no pension for former presidents at the time. Edith hoped to retire to Sagamore Hill and play the role of matriarch to the Roosevelt clan.

Before they departed from the White House, Edith was determined to provide her daughter Ethel with a social debut to rival Alice's. The debut was more elaborate and cost the family considerably more than the previous event, but it did not attract the media attention that Alice's party had. Ethel was Edith's daughter and had her mother's reserved nature and quiet demeanor. Edith followed the debut with an additional ball in Ethel's honor ten days after the formal occasion at the White House.

PREPARATIONS

Roosevelt decided that the best way for him to disappear from the public eye was to literally disappear from the country. He arranged to go on a safari through Kenya and Uganda. Roosevelt planned to gone for six months and to collect specimens for the Smithsonian Institute and the American Museum of Natural History which agreed to underwrite the expedition. Edith had mixed emotions about the trip. On one level, Edith realized that such an break would be good for her husband. She also understood that Theodore's restlessness would not allow him to be comfortable confined at Sagamore Hill for any length of time. Furthermore, the publishing company Scribner's offered Roosevelt a considerable amount of money for an account of his journey. Nevertheless, Edith was worried about her husband's health, especially the potential that he might contract a tropical disease. She also wished that Theodore would spend more time with her after he left office. After Roosevelt arranged to take a doctor with him on the safari, Edith acquiesced.

In preparation for his departure, Theodore handpicked William Howard Taft to succeed him. Taft was the Secretary of War under Roosevelt and a friend of the President's. Following an effort to convince Roosevelt to run for a third term at the Republican National Convention at Chicago in June of 1908, Taft was nominated as the Party's candidate. Although Theodore had publically announced that he did not want a third term, many close to him, including Edith, realized that he secretly hoped that the convention would draft him for another run. Edith had mixed emotions, but decided that she was ready to return to private life. Because of his pubic pronouncements, Roosevelt felt he had to accept Taft as the Party's nominee and on the surface supported the nomination.[2] After the convention, the President threw himself into his continuing effort to battle monopolies and corporate trusts. Meanwhile, Edith found a new friend in the person of Archibald Willingham Butt who was appointed Roosevelt's military aide. Butt became Edith's campion and confidant. His letters would later serve as a useful source of information about the personality and character of Edith.

On November 3, 1908, largely because of Roosevelt's endorsement, Taft was elected president. The actual transition proved to be difficult. The incoming First Lady, Helen Taft, stood in sharp contrast to Edith. While Edith was self-reserved and stood in the background of her husband's political career, Helen Taft was aggressive and actively influenced her husband's path to the White House. Helen planned a variety of changes to White House protocol and ceremony. While these were many minor alterations, they irked Edith. She was afraid that the members of the White House staff who she had grown close to over the years would not appreciate nor like the new First Lady's changes. In one of her last acts, she made arrangements to promote many of her favorite members of the staff.

During the weeks leading up to Taft's inauguration, Edith worked diligently to prepare the White House for its new occupants. She was particularly interested in ensuring that Helen would not have anything to complain about or belittle her for. As Edith had done when she left the governor's mansion in New York, Edith arranged a walk through tour with the incoming First Lady. The Tafts were invited to dine with the Roosevelts and spend the night in the White House on the eve of the inauguration. In the midst of the tour of the mansion, the incoming First Lady remarked for all to hear that "I would have put that table over there."[3] During the dinner, guests reported that in spite of her usual reserved manner, Edith was overcome with emotion following a speech by a her husband.

---

[2] Brands, p. 626.

[3] Sferrazza, p. 353.

The Roosevelt's departure was not without some controversy. Edith wished to take a small sofa that she had purchased in 1901 with her when she left the White House. When the newspapers discovered this, they published a series of articles critical of the First Lady. The reports implied that Edith was taking items without paying for them. Edith also took a pair of decorative figurines with her, but these were personal gifts that aroused little controversy.

Theodore and Kermit embarked on their safari on March 23, 1909, only a few weeks after the elder Roosevelt left office. While her husband was gone, Edith oversaw the household and took care of the children. She also managed the considerable correspondence that the family received (some 15,000 letters in the first few weeks after Roosevelt left office). While he was gone, Roosevelt asked that Archie Butt look in on Edith. Edith sincerely enjoyed Archie's company and he kept her informed of the happenings and gossip of Washington.

Edith did not intend to spend the entire time that Theodore was gone at Sagamore Hill. Instead, she had made plans to meet her husband in Europe. She left five months prior to the scheduled rendevous and undertook a tour of Europe with Ethel, Archie and Quentin (Ted had graduated from Harvard and begun to work). In July, Edith and her children met Emily for a few weeks. After an extended tour of Europe, Edith and the children met Roosevelt on March 14, 1910 in the Sudan. The family returned to tour Europe where they were received enthusiastically by heads of state and the general public. The tour was climaxed on May 5, when Theodore delivered his Nobel Prize speech. On May 16, Taft cabled Roosevelt to ask him to represent the United States at the funeral of King Edward VII of Great Britain. While he was in Great Britain, Roosevelt was asked to make a number of addresses and Both Oxford and Cambridge awarded him honorary degrees.

BACK INTO THE FRAY

The Roosevelts returned to the United States on June 18, 1910. Theodore was met by a hero's welcome. During his absence, the former president's popularity had increased. Taft's own political fortunes were in decline and there was already discussion of an effort to draft Roosevelt to run for the presidency in 1912. Edith and Theodore also returned to find Ted engaged to Eleanor Alexander. Edith was pleased with the choice. On June 20, the two were married and then moved to California where Ted began a career with the Hartford Carpet Company.

However, even as she celebrated the wedding, political storms began to gather around her husband. Since he had left office, Roosevelt perceived that a rift had emerged between himself and Taft. In many ways the gulf between the two was as much the fault of Roosevelt as it was of Taft. Roosevelt felt slighted that Taft had replaced a number of his Cabinet appointments when he became President. Taft had pledged to retain most of the Roosevelt Administration, but he naturally desired to appoint his own people to certain positions. Roosevelt also felt that the reformist policies that he had initiated were being abandoned by the Party. Meanwhile, within the Republican Party, many of the former President's supporters had never really given their loyalty to Taft. The Republican progressives wanted Roosevelt to return to the helm of the Party.

Roosevelt still retained his youthful energy and Edith realized that he had few outlets for his talents. He had begun his editorial work and initiated several book projects, but Roosevelt still seemed bored. After revolution broke out in Mexico, Roosevelt even volunteered to raise a division to fight if necessary. Edith feared that this boredom would draw her husband back into politics. Within weeks of his return, Roosevelt had begun to meet with Republican leaders and even attempted to gain the chairmanship of the New York State Republican Convention. That he was denied this honor rankled Roosevelt. The former president felt torn because he believed that it was his duty to support Taft, but there was increasing pressure from both within and outside of the Party for him to reenter the political fray at the national level. Roosevelt was astute even to understand that he could potentially split the Republican Party into two camps–the progressives that supported him and the conservatives that supported Taft. On the other hand, public pressure seemed to be mounting for a Roosevelt run for the presidency in 1912.

Roosevelt could have ended the speculation over his candidacy with a few well-chosen pronouncements. His work with *The Outlook* was going well and in 1911 he became a vice president of the American Historical Association (he was elected president of the organization the following year). He was also engaged in fundraising efforts on behalf of his favorite philanthropic endeavors, including the Smithsonian Institute. On another front, Ted and Eleanor had given Edith and Theodore a granddaughter, Grace Roosevelt, who was born in August of 1911.

However, the Democrats had swept the midterm elections in 1910 leading to additional pressure for Roosevelt to return to national politics. Many Republicans began to openly criticize Taft who most blamed for the electoral defeats. They also worried that a second Taft run for the presidency would lead to Democratic control of both Congress and the Presidency. Roosevelt found himself bombarded with calls from leading members of the Party and newspapers across the nation to run in 1912. Meanwhile, he sheepishly worked to keep his options open while nominally supporting Taft. Roosevelt let it be known that he would only consider another run if it was the will of the people. In a letter, Roosevelt declared that "My anxieties are in this order . . . not to be nominated if it can be honorably avoided . . . and . . . if nominated, to have it . . . clear that it is because . . . the public wishes me to serve them for their purpose."[4]

Edith eyed these events nervously. She strenuously objected to any effort by Theodore to reenter national politics. She wished that her husband would adjust to retirement and enjoy the public acclaim and adoration from the geographical distance of Oyster Bay. Also, Edith was as loyal to the Republican Party as her husband, perhaps even more so, and she dreaded the idea that Theodore might be the cause of a split in the Party. Edith repeatedly counseled her husband not to run. Besides the degree of political uncertainty, Edith faced other crises. On September 30, while riding with her husband, she was thrown from her horse and knocked unconscious. She remained in a coma for a day and a half and then suffered blinding headaches for several weeks thereafter. She also lost her sense of smell and her appetite and doctors were fearful that the disability might be permanent. However, Edith soon began to recover and regain her strength and senses. By November, Edith was up and about. The experience seems to have caused a great deal of reflection on the part of Theodore. The reminder of mortality may have been partially responsible for Roosevelt's later decision to run again for the presidency.

On December 2, the couple celebrated their twenty-fifth wedding anniversary. Edith had much to feel proud of both as a mother and a grandmother and she sincerely enjoyed the gathering of her family. Her two eldest children were married, although she was concerned that Alice and Nick had not had any children yet. Kermit was now at Harvard and Archie and

---

[4] Owen Wister, *Roosevelt: The Story of a Friendship, 1880-1919* (New York: Macmillan, 1930), p. 287.

Quentin would enter college soon. Ethel was twenty and likely to become engaged before too much longer. Since her recovery, Edith and Theodore had spent a considerable amount of time together and for Edith it seemed a return to their younger days. The period brought out the playfulness in Edith and when one prank was misunderstood by the French Ambassador who was at Sagamore Hill, Theodore pointed out "No, my dear Ambassador, people think I have a good-natured wife, but she has a humor which is more tyrannical than half the tempestuous women of Shakespeare."[5] Unfortunately for Edith, the family occasion proved to be the proverbial clam before the storm and by the beginning of 1912, Roosevelt had essentially begun to campaign for the presidency.

Edith was quietly furious at her husband. When it became apparent that Theodore intended to run in 1912, Edith muted her criticisms but made sure that her husband remained aware of her opposition. As more people visited Sagamore Hill in a concerted effort to convince him to run for the presidency, Edith left for New York in February. While ostensibly she left in order to attend a variety of events, including several operas and new plays, Edith realized that her influence on her husband was insignificant on political matters and she did not want to be around when he made his final decision– which she already assumed would be to launch a new campaign. Edith followed her New York escape with a journey to South America. Accompanied by Ethel, Edith visited a variety of areas, including Costa Rica, Panama and the British colony of Tobago. While she was on this voyage, Theodore announced his candidacy.

Roosevelt's decision created tensions with his friend Henry Cabot Lodge and caused problems for his son-in-law, Nick Longworth. Both were among the more conservative members of the Party, but their personal allegiances to Roosevelt prevented them from opposing the former president. As the campaign progressed, the rhetoric grew increasingly bitter. Taft sought to utilize the machinery of the Republican Party and political influence to secure the nomination while Roosevelt believed he could bypass the party bosses and appeal directly to the people. Taft accused Roosevelt of being a demagogue and Roosevelt countered with assertions that the current president was lazy and unfit for office. As the state primaries unfolded, both candidates scored

---

[5] Archibald W. Butt, *Taft and Roosevelt* (New York: Doubleday, 1930), pp. 829-832; quoted in Brands, p. 696.

victories. Taft used the state political machine to secure a victory in New York, while Taft's home state of Ohio went for Roosevelt. The West supported Roosevelt, but the more conservative South supported Taft. The battleground states were in the Northeast. By the time the primaries and caucuses ended, Roosevelt had 1,157,397 primary votes. Taft had only garnered 761,716. Once the convention votes began to be counted, Roosevelt found that he was only 70 votes short of the nomination.

Edith did not participate in her husband's campaigning. The spring of 1912 brought a series of misfortunes to her. Tensions between Edith and Alice again surfaced over the unwillingness of the daughter's husband to support either Taft or his father-in-law. Meanwhile, she received news that her close friend Archibald Butt had perished in April during the sinking of the *Titanic*. Also, Edith's friend, the historian Henry Adams, suffered a stroke during this period.

In June of 1912, Edith and Theodore arrived in Chicago, the site of the Republican National Convention. The former president found that many of his delegates were disputed and the Taft-controlled Convention Committee refused to seat many of Roosevelt's supporters. With this lock-out, Taft was able to win the nomination. Roosevelt's supporters cried "treachery" and most bolted from the convention. Many members of the Party sought to devise a compromise, but Roosevelt felt that his personal honor and the integrity of the Party had been affronted by Taft and the party bosses. On June 22, progressive members of the Republican Party held a counter convention to form a new "Progressive Party" and nominate Roosevelt as their candidate. Ten days later in Baltimore, Woodrow Wilson was nominated as the presidential candidate of the Democratic Party.

The new Progressive Party held a formal convention during the first weeks of August. On Wednesday the seventh, Roosevelt was officially nominated as the Party's candidate. He immediately through himself into the campaign with his usual vigor. Roosevelt attempted to present Taft and Wilson as insiders who were beholden to entrenched corporate and political interests. Unlike his previous campaigns, Roosevelt infused his campaign speeches with a high degree of morality. He likened the campaign to a religious crusade to free the nation of the political parasites that had prevented reform and stolen his nomination. He crisscrossed the nation delivering speeches and making appearances. Edith remained in New York.

On October 14, while in Milwaukee, Roosevelt was shot at close range by a disgruntled bar owner, John Schrank, who had held a grudge against the former police commissioner. A folded copy of his speech and his eyeglasses case which were both in his breast pocket slowed the bullet, preventing a serious injury. Although his aides tried to rush him to the hospital, Roosevelt realized he was not badly wounded and insisted on giving the speech. He even insisted that the would-be assassin not be harmed by the police and his supporters. Theodore began his speech by stating

> Friends, I shall ask you to be as quiet as possible . . . I don't know whether you fully understand that I have just been shot; but it takes more than that to kill a Bull Moose . . . . The bullet is in me now, so that I cannot make a very long speech, but I will try my best.[6]

Roosevelt opened his jacket so that the crowd could see his blood-stained shirt. He went on to give a rousing and powerful speech which lasted for an hour and a half. His reference to the Bull Moose caught the public's imagination and his new political party came to be referred to as the "Bull Moose" Party.

Edith received news of the assassination attempt while she was at a theater in New York. The episode confirmed her worst fears about her husband's political involvement. She left New York and along with Ted and Ethel went to Chicago the next day. Alice had been in Cincinnati and arrived at the hospital before Edith and the rest of the family. There she found that her father "looked surprisingly well, though obviously uncomfortable, and [he] said what an amazingly interesting experience it had been."[7] When she arrived, Edith immediately took charge of the situation. She established control over who could see Theodore and took charge of access by the press. With just two weeks to go before the election, Theodore returned to Oyster Bay. He was only able to manage two short speeches before election day.

When the election returns came in, Wilson won the election by a landslide in the Electoral College. Wilson received 6.3 million votes, Roosevelt 4.1 million and Taft 3.4 million. Alice's husband also lost his congressional seat. Roosevelt seemed to take the defeat in stride. Publically, he claimed to be proud of the impact that the Progressives had on the issues and the election.

---

[6] Brands, p. 721.

[7] Longworth, p. 217.

He also pronounced himself eager for another try in 1916. Meanwhile the former president returned to his writing. Edith spent the next few months working to help Theodore overcome his muted disappointment.

Chapter 9

LIFE ON THE OUTSIDE

L ife at Sagamore Hill returned to a settled pattern following the defeat in the presidential election. Theodore involved himself in a variety of writing projects Beginning in February 1913, he began to publish chapters from his autobiography in the journal *Outlook*. These installments were simultaneously published by a number of newspapers and other weeklies. In the work he alternatively praised the virtues of what he termed the "strenuous life" and wrote quite movingly of his devotion to Edith and their family and their importance to him. The essays were very successful and along with a slew of other writings, Theodore was able to gain a substantial annual income. Meanwhile, Roosevelt kept himself politically active by roundly criticizing the Wilson Administration at every chance. He was especially critical of the foreign policy and Secretary of State William Jennings Bryan.

By the winter of 1912-1913, Theodore had been home with Edith at Sagamore Bay for a longer period of time than at any other point in their marriage. As had been her habit, Edith oversaw the management of the household and the family's affairs while Theodore worked on his writing. However, a number of family occasions and crises emerged which prevented Edith from fully enjoying her time with her husband. Ted and his family had moved from California to New York City. Once back in New York, Ted had begun to drink heavily on occasion, prompting both Edith and Theodore to worry that Ted might meet a similar fate as Roosevelt's brother Elliot who had died of alcoholism. When Ted missed Christmas with the family and instead spent the holiday lunch at the New York club the Ritz, Edith felt that her son had completely gone over the edge.

Although Edith was deeply troubled by Ted's drinking, she received welcome news in the spring of 1913. Ethel had fallen in love with Richard Derby, a doctor who practiced at the Roosevelt Hospital in New York. Richard, or "Dick" as he was known to his friends, was a decade older than Ethel, but he was a successful doctor with a significant income. Edith initially thought him to be "taciturn and ill-at-ease," but she later reversed her opinion and decided that he was just quite and shy.[1] Meanwhile Theodore heartily endorsed the marriage. Arrangements were made for the ceremony to take place in April.

The two were married on April 4, 1913 at a church at Oyster Bay. Alice traveled from Ohio for the ceremony, but her husband declined to attend. This was a reflection of Nick's continuing animosity toward Theodore whom he blamed for the loss of his congressional seat. Alice described the wedding in the following manner: "Ethel was married in the little church in the village, with breakfast at Sagamore afterward. There were pretty bridesmaids, masses of spring flowers, rafts of friends–it was a perfect spring wedding."[2] Following the wedding, the couple departed for Europe for their honeymoon.

Not long after the wedding, Edith received word that her sister had appendicitis. She departed for Europe and met Ethel and her husband on June 10, 1913, in Lausanne, Switzerland where Emily's surgery was scheduled. The operation was a success and after a few weeks of recovery, Edith and Emily traveled to the Mediterranean. While Edith was in Europe, the Roosevelt children spent the summer with Theodore. Archie and Quentin were home from school and Alice had decided to spend the summer in New York rather than Ohio. Ted and his family also spent considerable time at Sagamore Hill. The time spent together with his eldest son helped alleviate Theodore's concerns over Ted's drinking. As Edith, Ethel and Dick sailed back to New York, Theodore, Archie and Quentin set-off by train on a five-week-long tour of the American Southwest. The three visited the Grand Canyon and other areas of Arizona and Theodore met with several groups of his Rough Rider companions. Concurrently, Theodore made also plans to travel to South America to deliver a series of speeches and lectures and to explore the Amazon rainforest. Roosevelt planned to travel by ship to Rio de Janeiro, and then explore Brazil, Argentina, Paraguay and Chile. The American Museum

---

[1] Morris, p. 394.
[2] Longworth, p. 227.

of Natural History and the government of Brazil agreed to provide financial backing. Roosevelt also arranged to have Scribner's publish a series of articles that he would write.

When Edith returned, she discovered her husband's plans and after considerable lobbying on the part of Theodore, she agreed to accompany the expedition as far as Rio de Janeiro. He used the financial incentive of the essays as a justification for the journey. Upon her return form Europe, Edith also learned that Ethel was now pregnant and she determined to return in time for the birth. Edith traveled with Theodore, her son Kermit, and a cousin, Margaret Roosevelt to South America. The party arrived in Bahia, Brazil on October 18. Edith and Theodore thoroughly enjoyed the ship voyage and their time together in Rio. Along with various dignitaries, the family celebrated Theodore's fifty-fifth birthday. To add to the generally festive mood of the Roosevelts, Kermit received news that Belle Willard, the daughter of the American Ambassador to Spain, had agreed to marry him.

On November 26, Edith and Margaret left the adventurers and set sail for New York. They had decided to stop briefly in Panama on the return voyage. While there Margaret became stricken with typhoid. With three weeks, the young woman was dead. The loss of her companion deeply troubled Edith and cast a pall over the entire journey. To compound matters, soon after her return to New York in January of 1914, Edith was informed that Grandma Lee, Alice's maternal grandmother, had died.

Instead of returning to Sagamore Hill, Edith spent the next few months helping Ethel prepare for the birth of her child. On March 7,1914, Ethel gave birth to a son who was christened Richard Junior, in honor of his father. Although the excitement of the pregnancy and the delivery had kept Edith distracted from thoughts of her husband, she had really begun to miss Theodore and worry about his safety. And there was reason to worry. Unbeknownst to Edith, toward the end of the expedition, Theodore re-injured the leg that he had originally hurt in 1902 in the streetcar crash. The leg became infected and Theodore suffered from a recurring fever. Nonetheless, he pressed on with his characteristic will. Kermit described one episode

> There was one particularly black night . . . . We had been working through a series of rapids that seemed interminable. There would be a long carry, a mile or so clear going, and then more rapids.
> The fever was high and father was out of head. Doctor Cajazeira, who was one of the three Brazilian with us, divided with me the watch during the

night. The scene is vivid before me. The black rushing river with the great trees towering high above along the banks; the sodden earth under foot; for a few moments the stars would be shining, and then the sky would cloud over and the rain would fall in torrents, shutting out the sky and trees and river. Father first began with poetry; over and over again he repeated "In Xanadu did Kubla Khan a stately pleasure dome decree," then he started talking at random, but gradually he centered down to the question of supplies, which was, of course, occupying every's mind. Part of the time he knew that I was there, and he would then ask me if I thought Cherrie had had enough to eat to keep going. Then he would forget my presence and keep saying to himself: "I can't work now, so I don't need much food, but he and Cherrie have worked all day with the canoes, they must have part of mine."[3]

By the end of the journey, Theodore and his companions had covered 500 miles through the jungle in just over 60 days. Theodore returned to New York on May 19. A week later he was off to New York to deliver an address to the National Geographic Society. At the end of May, Roosevelt and Alice set sail for Europe to attend Kermit's wedding in Spain.

Edith did not attend the wedding. The combination of Margaret's unexpected death and her husband's long absence seemed to have taken their emotional toll on Edith. In addition, in her biography of the First Lady, Sylvia Jukes Morris suggests that Edith was experiencing menopause during this period.[4] While he was in Europe during the summer of 1914, Arch Duke Franz Ferdinand of Austria was assassinated. Few at the time realized the implications of the event, but by August of 1914, the great powers of Europe where at war.

LOOKING FOR A WAY BACK IN

When Roosevelt returned to New York at the end of that summer, many sought to draw him back into the political fray. The remnants of the Progressive Party wanted Roosevelt to lead them again in the presidential election of 1916. In the interim, Progressives in the state of New York were trying to convince Roosevelt to run in the 1914 gubernatorial race. Edith vehemently opposed any return to politics, fearing for her husband's safety and his health. He was still suffering from the effects of the fever he had

---

[3] Kermit Roosevelt, *The Happy Hunting Grounds* (New York: Scribner's, 1921), pp. 46-8.
[4] Morris, p. 403.

acquired in the jungle. Edith had doctors summed to examine Theodore and they concluded that his voice and constitution would not stand the strain of repeated campaign speeches. In fact, he was ordered by the doctors to rest for a minimum of four months. Therefore, he declined to run for the governorship. It was probably fortunate that Roosevelt did not run, for Wilson had captured the support of most of the nation's Progressives. In the 1914 midterm elections, the Progressive Party suffered enormous defeats at both the state and national level (the only major victory for the Party occurred in California where Roosevelt's running mate from the 1912 presidential election, Hiram Johnson, was elected governor).

In the wake of the elections, Roosevelt remained at Sagamore Hill and spent time with Edith, the children and grandchildren. He resigned from the journal *Outlook* in order to gain a three-year contract with the *Metropolitan Magazine*. The new post came with an annual salary of $25,000. Roosevelt had the contract set at three years because at its conclusion, Quentin would have graduated from Harvard, and the former President hoped to retire.

In spite of Edith's pleas, the war in Europe drew Roosevelt back into the political spotlight. He deeply disagreed with Wilson's neutrality policies and Roosevelt actively campaigned for American involvement on the side of the Allied powers. He wrote article after article in which he criticized the barbarity of the Germans for their use of unrestricted submarine warfare. Many of these essays were collected into a book published in 1915, *America and the World War*. He also let it be known that he intended to raise a cavalry division and fight if the United States was brought into the war. Edith continued to worry about her husband's health. The injury to his leg and the continuing impact of the jungle fever had significantly weakened his constitution.

As the 1916 presidential election approached, Edith convinced Theodore that the optimum method to remove himself from the political machinations of the nation was to leave the United States. Consequently, the two left for a six-month tour of the Caribbean. They left in February and while on their vacation, they received news that Kermit and Belle had a son, Kermit. Upon their return to New York, Edith and Theodore found there was still significant public pressure for him to run. Partially in a effort to deflect such sentiment and partially in an attempt to redeem himself in the eyes of the Republican Party, Roosevelt began to formally campaign on behalf of the Republican candidate, Charles Evans Hughes. Edith was pleased with her husband's efforts since they meant that he clearly was not going to run himself and she had never really been comfortable with the defection from the Republican Party. She also shared her husband's deep dislike for Wilson–although her enmity was based on the belief that the President was too liberal, while Theodore's animosity sprung form his perception that Wilson was a coward because of his handling of the World War. He wrote to his friend Cabot Lodge that he thought Wilson "yellow all through in the presence of danger, either physically or morally."[5]

In addition to his political efforts to defeat Wilson, Roosevelt also campaigned in support of military preparedness. This included support for his former commanding officer Leonard Wood in the general's effort to establish voluntary training centers for prospective soldiers. The camps were private and not part of the regular military. At Wood's camp in Plattsburg, New York, Roosevelt was joined by his sons Ted, Archie and Quentin. He was proud of the manner in which his sons took to the military life, and especially proud that the regular officers in the camp stated that Archie already had the military knowledge and leadership to be a captain the Army.[6]

Wilson was reelected in 1916, but Roosevelt was cheered when his nephew, Corrine's son Theodore Robinson, was elected a senator from New York. By the winter of 1917, it appeared that American involvement in the war was imminent. Germany had declared a policy of unrestricted submarine warfare and in return, Wilson had broken-off diplomatic relations. Sensing the coming crisis. Edith and Theodore canceled a planned Caribbean vacation and a future six-month tour of the Far East. When war was declared on April 6, 1917, Roosevelt set-off for the White House in order to offer his services. He specifically requested permission to command a division in Europe. After meeting with Wilson, Roosevelt was informed that his services were not needed. Officially, his limited military service and his age were cited as the reasons for his rejection. However, both Theodore and Edith were convinced that Wilson's decision was entirely political in that he did not want to allow Roosevelt any more political capital. Roosevelt's desire to be involved in the war even led him to inquire of his friend Spring-Rice if it would be feasible

---

[5] Theodore Roosevelt to Henry Cabot Lodge, March 1, 1917, Morrison.

[6] Brands, pp. 757-58.

for the former President to raise a division of American soldiers to fight under the Canadian flag (a request which Spring-Rice politely rebuffed).[7]

In the middle of the war-mania, Archie announced his intention to marry. On April 14, he married Grace Lockwood in a ceremony in Boston. The wedding provided some minor comfort for Edith who had begun to worry deeply about her sons. Theodore was relentless in his efforts to have his male children fight in World War I, especially if he could not. Ted and Archie were granted commissions in the American Expeditionary Force under General John "Black Jack" Pershing. Meanwhile, Quentin gained a commission as an aviator. Kermit did not have the same experience as his brothers and was unable to gain a commission in the U.S. Army, but Theodore managed to gain him a position in the British Army in the Middle East. By the end of the summer, all of Edith's sons had left for the war.

She was almost consumed with fear for her sons. Theodore began traveling the nation to give speeches on behalf of the war effort, leaving Edith essentially alone at Sagamore Hill. She tried to provide comfort and support for her daughter-in-laws and discovered that before Quentin left for France he was secretly engaged to Flora Payne Whitney. Flora began to spend considerable with Edith and they were soon joined by Ethel, whose husband left to serve in the medical corps in Europe. In an effort to occupy their time, Theodore arranged to take Edith, Ethel and Flora on a speaking tour he made in Canada. After the tour, Theodore was admitted to Roosevelt Hospital where he had to have surgery in order to remove several abscesses. Although the surgery was successful, Theodore developed an infection in his left ear which ultimately left him deaf on that side. He languished for three weeks before he recovered enough to resume activities. While he was relatively young, Edith worried that her husband's growing weight and declining health were taking its toll on his physical stamina.

While still dealing with the emotional strains of Theodore's surgery, Edith received a succession of bad news. First, Cecil Spring-Rice, friend to both Roosevelts, died in the winter of 1918. His death was followed by that of Henry Adams. Then on March 13, news came that Archie had been badly wounded in France. Although he survived and was awarded the Croix de Guerre, Archie suffered debilitating injuries to his knee and arm. Meanwhile Kermit had won the British Military Cross for bravery and as a result he was

---

[7] Ibid., p. 778.

allowed to transfer to the U.S. Army with the rank of captain. For his part Ted had been promoted to lieutenant-colonel, and awarded both the Silver Star and the Croix de Guerre for leading his men in an attack after he had been gassed. Finally, Edith and Theodore received news which devastated them. On July 16, 1918, while engaged in air combat over France, Quentin was shot down. After four days of agonizing uncertainty, they received confirmation that their son had been killed.

Both parents were devastated. Worse yet, they received news that Ted had been badly wounded again. Then Archie came home after his wounds necessitated his separation from active service. Archie's wounds would trouble him for the remainder of his life. Throughout this period, Edith was the rock of stability for the family. Theodore relied heavily on her as he tried to maintain his public composure. He understood how hard it was for Edith, he wrote to Kermit and described how he sensed that "At home she [Edith] sees Quentin in every room."[8] Nonetheless, the death of Quentin would ultimately harm Theodore the most. He never really recovered from his son's death.

The November congressional elections resulted in the Republicans regaining control of both houses of Congress. Momentum seemed to be building toward another run for the presidency. Roosevelt was still the nation's best-known and most popular Republican. During the build-up to the elections, Roosevelt and Taft had even reconciled and campaigned together to defeat the Democrats. However, he had begun to suffer from crippling arthritis. Edith noticed that his health seemed to be declining rapidly, but he refused to slow his pace. On November 11, 1918, Roosevelt had to be taken to the hospital because of his arthritis. His condition reached the point that he had to use a wheelchair. Little could be done for Theodore's pain. Edith remained by his side throughout the period. She managed to convince the hospital staff that her husband should be allowed to go home for the Christmas holiday. Theodore enjoyed Christmas at Sagamore Hill. Alice, Ethel and Archie were there (Ted and Kermit remained in Europe on duty). But all noticed how much their father had deteriorated physically. He now spent most of his time lying in bed or on a sofa, except for periods when Edith would drive him around the estate. Roosevelt had become increasingly reflective of his life and often spoke more of his past glories than of any future prospects.

---

[8] Theodore Roosevelt to Kermit Roosevelt, August 10, 1918, Theodore Roosevelt Collection.

Again and again his thoughts returned to his wartime experiences. Writing about Roosevelt's romanticism, biographer H. W. Brands summarized the former President's sentiments in the following manner:

> He [Roosevelt] had joined the army to test himself, to see if he measured up to the heroic ideal he had constructed in his imagination. The test, the supreme test of fire, had come, and he had indeed measured up. The inner glow of satisfaction that his achievement produced would never dim. Two decades later, only months before he died and after many intervening accomplishments of far greater worth to the world at large, he could look back and declare, "San Juan was the great day of my life."[9]

The dimming of the ex-President's internal fire and energy was a foreshadowing of the end. Roosevelt had never recovered from the death of Quentin and his thoughts also turned to family and Sagamore Hill. Just before Roosevelt's death, Edith wrote Ted

> Father was in your old nursery and loved the view, of which he spoke, and as it got dusk he watched the dancing flames and spoke of the happiness of being home, and made little plans for me. I think he had made up his mind that he would have to suffer for some time to come and with his high courage had adjusted himself to bear it. He was very sweet all day. Since Quentin was killed he has been sad, only Ethel's little girl had the power to make him merry.[10]

Later that evening he surprised Edith by pronouncing "I wonder if you will ever know how much I love Sagamore Hill."[11]

On the evening of January 5, 1919, Theodore told Edith that he had problems breathing. After he went to sleep, she checked on him several times. Although his breathing was labored, he seemed fine. Edith was awoken at around 4:15 in the morning by Theodore's nurse who informed her that Theodore had stopped breathing. Doctors were called in, but the former President had indeed slipped away. His death was attributed to a coronary embolism.

---

[9] Brands, p. 357.

[10] Quoted in Hermann Hagedorn, *The Roosevelt Family of Sagamore Hill* (New York: Macmillan Company, 1954), p. 424.

[11] Ibid.

In spite of her deep personal grief, Edith continued to function with the efficiency and purpose which had marked her life. She informed the children and then called Corrine at 6:00 in the morning. During the conversation, Corrine recalled that Edith's voice was "gentle and self-controlled, though vibrant with grief, told me that he was gone, and that she wanted me to come at once to Sagamore."[12] The passage of Theodore brought the two old friends back together and their shared grief was mollified by each other's company. Ted and Kermit were still in Europe and Archie cabled his brothers with the simple phrase "the old lion is dead."

True to her private nature, Edith wished to avoid the sensationalism and media involvement that a public ceremony would entail. Instead, she chose to have a small and unpretentious funeral. Many of Theodore's friends, political allies and the public in general were surprised since the simplicity of the occasion seemed to run counter to the larger-than-life presence that the former President had been during his lifetime. Sagamore Hill was inundated with cables and condolence messages from around the world and from both the average citizen and heads of state.

Roosevelt was laid to rest on January 8, 1919. Edith remained in the house at Oyster Bay during Theodore's simple funeral which was held at the Christ Church Cemetery in town. Roosevelt was buried in a hillside plot that he and Edith had chosen several years prior. Although the funeral was relatively small, the ceremony was attended by numerous dignitaries and officials, including former president Taft who openly wept at the end of the ceremony.

---

[12] Robinson, p. 365.

Chapter 10

LIFE AFTER THEODORE

The depth of personal grief that Edith underwent during this period was almost unfathomable. Within a six-month period, Edith lost her son Quentin and her husband. In addition, two of her other sons had been badly wounded during World War I. For most of her existence Edith had centered her life around Theodore and his loss left a deep void. Her daughter Ethel wrote that "She [Edith] has so lived for Father that I almost believe she will die too."[1] Immediately after her husband's funeral, Edith left Sagamore Hill and traveled to Bamie's house. Just as Corrine had helped her through the funeral, Bamie aided Edith through the difficult period following the ceremony. By this point in her life Bamie also suffered from arthritis and was confined to a wheel chair and it pained Edith to see what her old friend was experiencing. After the initial period of reconciliation between Edith and the sisters, they grew further-and-further apart and corresponded less through the years.

With her recent losses, Edith felt the need to be with her two sons who were still in Europe. Consequently, she arranged passage to France and set sail on February 5, 1919. Ted and Kermit met Edith at La Harve and the group traveled to Paris where Emily awaited them. On February 18, the group visited Quentin's grave, where Edith arranged for a monument to be constructed. Edith planned to spend the winter and spring with her sister, but the long-running tensions between the two led Edith to travel back to New York. She arrived on May15, 1919.

---

[1] Caroli, *Roosevelt Women*, p. 206.

Toward the end of his life, Theodore had become fairly wealthy for his day. In addition to the family's investments, Theodore's income had been greatly enhanced by his writing. Theodore's death led industrial multi-millionaire Andrew Carnegie to establish a trust fund for presidential widows, including Edith. The fund paid the widows an annual income of $5,000. This was followed by another annual pension of $5,000 which was provided by Congress. In addition, Theodore had a generous life insurance policy. All told, Edith would remain financially secure for the remainder of her life and pass on a significant inheritance to her surviving children and charitable organizations.

TRAVEL

Without the presence of Theodore, Sagamore Hill did not hold the same charms for Edith. She had traveled extensively during her life, but after Theodore's death she traveled even more frequently. Following her trip to France in 1919, Edith embarked on a journey to South America with Kermit. The two visited Argentina, Chile and Brazil. Edith developed a habit of frequenting warmer climates during the winter months. This allowed her to be gone during the gloomiest time of the year, both emotionally and in terms of weather.

She also began exploring ever more exotic locations. She seemed determined to spend as much time as possible away from the family home and see the rest of the world that she had been reading about for all of these years. Consequently, many of the locations she visited were divided between those areas where her husband or other family members had been (including Alice and her sons) or those areas that formed the background for some of her favorite works. Travel also provided a welcome distraction from the complications of family life. Edith would later refer to her travels as the "odyssey of a grandmother."[2]

The year 1922, saw Edith in the Caribbean where she visited Grenada and British Guiana among other destinations. In 1922, she and Archie journeyed to France and then to Germany and Great Britain. In Paris, Edith, who was fluent in French, enjoyed the Parisian cafes and shops and was particularly delighted by the city's numerous small book stores where she purchased a number of rare or older works. From Paris, the two went to Germany. Edith and Kermit then flew to London. This marked Edith's first experience with flight. There were problems with the flight which encountered stormy weather and led them to change planes. Edith never became comfortable with flying and preferred earth-bound forms of transportation. The European tour was immediately succeeded by a voyage to South Africa. Once there, Edith spent a considerable amount of time on the beaches of the Cape of Good Hope and seemed to regain much of her balance. The experience may have marked the real beginning of her healing process after the loss of Theodore.

The South African voyage was followed a year later by another journey to Europe. While in Europe, Edith visited Emily in Italy and then embarked on a voyage to Brazil. She and Kermit subsequently planned a two-month around the world epic voyage which included stops in Hawaii and Japan. While in Japan, Edith survived an earthquake on January 15, and was enthusiastically received by Japanese officials and the people because of her husband's role in negotiating an end to the Russo-Japanese War in 1905. Kermit and his mother then journeyed on to China and undertook a 6,000 jaunt on the trans-Siberian railway to Moscow. In both China and Russia, Edith's political conservatism was reinforced by the chaos and famine that had resulted from the recent revolutions. Edith was particularly struck by the poverty and destitution of the people and the degree of political repression. The fear of the people of the Soviet government was particularly poignant and confirmed her opinion of the dangers of communism.

In addition to her international travels, Edith initiated an annual pilgrimage of the soul. In 1922, she led a group of family members and friends to her husband's grave. At first, she would march with the group to the grave and lay a memorial wreath, but as the years past Edith continued to partake in the odyssey although she could walk along with her friends and family. After the group visited the grave they would return to Sagamore Hill where they would read aloud from Theodore's works and engage in discussions of his policies and impact. Participants in the event often described Edith relaying some personal or little known anecdote about Theodore. For her, the process was "cathartic" and provided a release for her

---

[2] Prindiville, p. 201.

feelings and emotions toward her husband.[3] Edith would participate in this annual event for the next twenty years.

In 1926, Edith undertook a journey to Mexico where she explored the Maya ruins in the Yucatán Peninsula. She then ventured on to Argentina. A year later she published a travel book along with Kermit, Belle, and her son-in-law, Dick Derby. The work was entitled *Cleared for Strange Ports*. The work described the journeys of the family and the many lands that they had visited. This was followed by a number of travel articles for the journal *Scribner's*. There was considerable sentiment for Edith to pen a memoir of her life and experiences as First Lady. Instead, Edith wrote a genealogical history of the two sides of her family, the Carows and the Tylers. Kermit assisted his mother as she selected various works, including diaries and family journals, to include in the work which she titled *American Backlogs*. The book traced the family history of the Carows and the Tylers from the 1600s through the death of her grandfather Daniel Tyler in 1882. Although it was favorably reviewed by many newspapers and journals across the country, it did not sell well. However, Edith's main purpose was to relate the story of her family and she was pleased with the outcome of the work.

Even after she turned seventy in 1931, Edith continued her journeys with travels to South America, Europe and the Caribbean. However, by the late 1920s, Edith's health had begun to cause her problems. She had heart murmurs which she described as "heart attacks."[4] Her last significant voyage was to South America in 1935, although she spent a brief period in Haiti in 1939. Her condition and her general aversion to the public led Edith to search for a second home where she could avoid the often jumbled world of Sagamore Hill with its legions of relatives and children. She chose to return to her childhood home and the ancestral lands of her family, the Tylers. The former First Lady was able to purchase the home of one of her great-grandfathers which had been used as an inn for some time. The house was located in Brooklyn, Connecticut on two and a half acres of land. She formally acquired the title to the property on August 25, 1927. The house was large and roomy and Edith sincerely enjoyed her new purchase.

Edith would either travel overseas during the winter or spend it at Oyster Bay, but at various times in the summer and spring, she made the journey to

---

[3] Morris, p. 452.
[4] Ibid., p. 467.

Brooklyn with only her maid, cook and chauffeur. Her purchase surprised her family and friends. They were even more troubled by her desire to spend time in relative isolation. However, the house suited Edith's sense of privacy. After a lifetime in the pubic eye, the manor in Brooklyn allowed Edith her solitude and time for reflection. The home was also near Bamie's house, although the two saw each other only occasionally because of Bamie's increasing infirmity.

The house, which she renamed Mortlake Manor (as it was originally known), further provided an outlet for Edith to use her creative talents to redecorate and refurbish. Following Theodore's death, Edith had undertaken a variety of repairs and renovations at Sagamore Hill. However, as a tribute to her husband and in an effort not to upset her children, Edith kept the interior of the family estate more or less as it had been when Theodore roamed the halls. The constant remainders of her late husband at Sagamore may have also been a factor in her desire to purchase Mortlake Manor.

POLITICS

Throughout her husband's political career, Edith had remained in the background. However, after his death she began to become more of a presence in politics. Her increased visibility occurred for two reasons. First, Edith worked to support the political careers of her family and friends. Second, Edith's staunch support for the Republican national party led her to enter the political fray in order to defeat the Democratic Party whom she blamed for many of the country's problems. In the fall of 1919, Ted decided to campaign for the New York State assembly. On November 4, he was elected by an overwhelming margin. In spite of her grief, Edith found the time to lobby on behalf on her son. She took his election as a sign of the continuing popularity of the Roosevelt name and the legacy of her husband.

In 1920, Edith decided to become active in national politics. The way had already been opened by Corrine who had been selected to serve on the New York State Republican Committee. In spite of a variety of ailments, Corrine traveled across the United States campaigning on behalf of Republican candidates. At the 1920 party assembly Corrine became the first woman to address a Republican National Convention. Corrine's success and influence was a "model" for Edith.[5] The former First Lady added her own weight to the Republican cause during that year. In September she wrote a stirring essay for *The Woman-Republican* in which fervently endorsed the Republican ticket of Warren G. Harding and Calvin Coolidge. The essay contained many of the themes that Roosevelt had used during his career, including appeals to national pride and the need for political participation. The passage of the Nineteenth Amendment in September meant that women were eligible to vote in national elections and Edith was determined to impress upon her fellow women the need to support the Republican Party. Edith wrote that

> The country's vital need is the election of the Republican candidates, Warren G. Harding and Calvin Coolidge. Only will the full measure of Americanism in the next administration be attained if the people shall declare for the party which holds true nationalism as its high ideal . . . .
> The time appeals most strongly to the manhood and the womanhood of America. To woman more than ever before because to her has come the perfected opportunity to make her influence weighty in behalf of the nation . . . .
> Steadiness and staunchness of American purpose are obligatory if we would first bring back our country to its stable place and then by strong endeavor do all that can be done for peace and general welfare in all lands.[6]

The reference to "Americanism" is a direct relation to the last message that Theodore gave.[7] The essay was prepared by Theodore but read on January 5, 1919 by Henry C. Quimby because of the former president's infirmity. The theme of the address was "Standup for Americanism" and Edith clearly sought to tie her plea to the popular support for the deep patriotism of her late husband.

November of 1920, also saw Ted reelected to the state legislature. Then in March of 1921, Ted was appointed an Assistant Secretary of the Navy. Edith was proud that her eldest son was following in the footsteps of his father. In 1924, he resigned the post to run for governor of New York. However, he had been accused of involvement in the Teapot Dome Scandal and although he was able to prove his innocence, he lost the election. Edith was disappointed with the result and particularly furious that Ted's cousin Eleanor, wife of

---

[5] Caroli, p. 206.

[6] Quoted in Morris, pp. 447-48.

[7] Cheney, p. 133.

Franklin Delano Roosevelt, had actively campaigned to defeat him. Edith never forgave what she saw as a betrayal of the family and would work diligently to defeat Franklin when he was the vice-presidential nominee in the 1928 elections.

Edith worked to support Republican Herbert Hoover in the 1928 presidential elections. Her efforts seem to have been motivated as much by her staunch distaste for the Democratic Party as they were on behalf of her eldest son. Edith hoped that if elected Hoover would provide some political appointment for Ted. Her wishes came true and in 1929, Ted was appointed governor of Puerto Rico. As governor, Ted proved to be remarkably successful and this appointment was followed by a position as governor-general of the Philippines.

In 1932, Edith engaged in the most hard-fought political campaign that she had ever directly participated in. The Democrats had nominated Franklin to be their presidential candidate and Edith went to extraordinary lengths to defeat him. She made several addresses in support of Hoover, the climax of which was an appearance at Madison Square Garden just a little over a week before the election. During the speech, he praised Hoover's accomplishments and roundly criticized her relative. Nonetheless, the election's results were a foregone conclusion and Hoover was significantly defeated by Roosevelt.

Edith's last significant political act involved a speech which commemorated the adoption of the Constitution. The address was delivered on September 16, 1935 and broadcast nationwide.

FAMILY

Edith's sense of privacy had always been a major component of her personality. With the death of her husband, this concern over public scrutiny became even more heightened. In 1919, when the historian William Thayer began his authoritative work *Theodore Roosevelt: An Intimate Biography*, he found Edith reluctant to allow him access to private materials and had to turn to Corrine for help. In particular, Edith had refused Thayer permission to use numerous quotes from the private letters of the family. Corrine could not "understand how anyone, Mrs. Roosevelt or anyone else, has the right to object."[8] Like Corrine, Bamie and most of the family thought that Thayer's work would enhance the reputation of Roosevelt and enthusiastically cooperated with the author. Most were very careful not to offend Edith and as the years went by, members of the Roosevelt family were very hesitant to comment on the personal life of Edith and Theodore.

Ultimately, Edith did cooperate with her husband's many biographers, but only to a certain extent. The original episode with Thayer heightened her concerns over maintaining the integrity of her private life with Theodore. Edith was often asked to edit and provide copies of correspondence between Theodore and various figures. In order to ensure that her private correspondence with her husband was never revealed, she went through and destroyed a significant amount of the most personal letters and notes in 1923. The correspondence that she kept were those that related to the children or that were less personal in nature.

In 1924, Edith received the remarkable news that at age forty-one, Alice was pregnant. The news upset Edith who felt that Alice was too old for motherhood. Nonetheless, Edith traveled to Chicago in February, 1925. Alice gave birth to a daughter, Paulina, on February 14. Edith was sincerely relieved to see that Alice's and baby were both healthy following the delivery and hoped that the child would smooth some of the tensions between her stepdaughter and her husband. Alice's new baby raised the number of grandchildren to fifteen.

Of her children, Archie had become the one that Edith relied most upon. In 1921, he had purchases a home near Sagamore Hill and he spent considerably more time with Edith than did any of the other children through the 1920s and 1930s. Archie usually made Edith's travel arrangements and would take her to and pick her up form the dock during her journeys. He also was her frequent companion when she went to New York for the theater or musicals.

On April 2, 1931, Edith received word that Alice's husband Nick had died unexpectedly after contracting pneumonia. Edith traveled to Cincinnati to attend the funeral. Doubtless because of her experiences in losing Theodore, Edith proved to be a great comfort to Alice. The rapproachment between the two which had begun with the birth of Paulina was strengthened by Edith's

---

[8] Caroli, p. 204.

actions and much of the tensions of Alice's childhood faded away through the remaining years of Edith's life.

Although she was happy to be a comfort to Alice, Nick's death took an enormous emotional toll on Edith because it rekindled the emotions that surrounded Theodore's death. Her sadness was exacerbated in August of 1931 when she received news that Bamie had fallen into a coma. Edith rushed to be at her side, but Bamie died on August 25, without recovering consciousness. Edith was on her way back from a visit to Ted in the Philippines in February 1933, when she received word that Corrine had died. Despite the gap between the three former friends which emerged in their later lives, the deaths of her childhood companions filled Edith with a deep sense of isolation and grief.

FINAL YEARS

On November 12, 1935, Edith fell and broke her hip. The injury significantly slowed her down and it never completely healed, but in April of 1936, she was fitted with a brace which allowed her to walk. She traveled to the Gulf Coast of Florida the following year where she spent her time on the beaches of the Gulf of Mexico. Concern for her son Kermit had reached a significant level. He was depressed over his business career and the impact of the Great Depression and had begun to drink heavily. Meanwhile, Ted and Eleanor had decided to build a new home on the Oyster Bay estate. Completed in 1938, Old Orchard Bay was a massive mansion which Edith approved of, but found that there were growing tensions between her and her daughter-in-law. In the midst of construction of the new home Eleanor had even sent Edith a bill for $140 for a strand of trees which were planted between Sagamore Hill and the new house.[9]

In February of 1939, Edith received news that her sister Emily had contracted pneumonia. On March 19, Edith was informed that Emily had died. Edith's estrangement with Emily weighed heavily on her mind through her remaining years. She was especially upset that she had not seen her sister before her death. Even as she contemplated the recent losses in her life, events in Europe were about to dramatically expand her sorrow.

The outbreak of World War II in September of 1939, led Kermit to volunteer to serve in the British Army again. He fought in Norway and then

Egypt where he contracted malaria. The disease led to his discharge in 1941. Upon his return to the United States he began to drink even more heavily. In an effort to save him, it was arranged through the President that Kermit be commissioned a major in the U.S. Army and sent to Alaska where it was hoped he could recover. Meanwhile Ted had rejoined the American Army where he became a brigadier general in the infantry. Archie also persuaded the War Department to grant him a commission and rose to the rank of lieutenant-colonel by the end of the war. Several grandsons also served in the military. For Edith, the potential loss of another son to war was an onerous burden to bear during the war years.

Once in Alaska, Kermit again took to drink. There was little for him and his fellow officers to do, and the combination of alcohol and boredom left him deeply depressed. On June 4, 1943, Kermit committed suicide by shooting himself in the head with his service pistol. It was decided not to tell Edith or the public the circumstances of Kermit's death. Instead she was told that Kermit had died of heart problems. The loss of Kermit further ravaged Edith's emotional state, sending her into a deep depression. Interestingly, it was Alice who helped Edith through this period. Her stepdaughter came more frequently to Sagamore Hill and kept Edith informed of the political gossip of Washington and the news of the war.

In the spring and summer of 1944, Ted found himself in Great Britain preparing for the invasion of Normandy. His boat was one of the first ashore on June 6, when the invasion began. At age fifty-six, Ted was the oldest Allied soldier involved in the attack. For his bravery on Utah Beach, Ted was recommended for the Medal of Honor by General Omar Bradley. Unbeknownst to Edith, Ted had heart problems and had been advised by Army physicians to rest. However, he plunged on with characteristic Roosevelt vigor. On July 12, his exertions overtaxed his health and he died of a heart attack. Roosevelt was posthumously awarded the Medal of Honor and became the most decorated American soldier of World War II.

Ted's death led Edith to withdraw increasingly from contact with friends and family. The loss of three of her four sons in war devastated the elderly Edith. To compound matters, Archie was still serving in the Pacific theater where he had been wounded several times and awarded the Silver Star for gallantry. However, in January a recurrence of malaria led him to be

---

[9] Morris, p. 496.

transferred to California to recover. Although Edith worried about her son's disease, she was glad to see him removed from combat.

As she grew older, Edith's temperament worsened. She was often volatile and unpredictable. At one point she decided that she did not like the noise and exhaust of cars and required that family members park their cars some distance from Sagamore Hill and walk a lengthy trail to the main house. Her vindictiveness which had occasionally displayed itself in her younger days became more pronounced. The former First Lady who was noted for her grace would launch into angry tirades against those who she perceived had slighted her. She also acted petty toward the grandchildren when they displeased her. Edith would often give mementos to her grandchildren and then ask for them back when they made her angry and at times for no apparent reason at all. It is likely that Edith had begun to loss her mental faculties. For instance, in 1945, when Ted's son Quentin II visited Sagamore Hill, Edith mistook him for her Quentin.[10] As time went by, Edith's two remaining children, Ethel and Archie, came to disagree on how to care for Edith. Ethel continued to play the role of dutiful daughter. She accepted Edith's personality quirks and her temper with a grace that was remarkable under the circumstances.[11]

As the war ended in Europe and then Japan, Edith's health began to decline rapidly. She seemed to lose much of her interest in affairs. Nonetheless, she continued to engage in correspondence and especially liked to write answers to queries concerning her late husband. Edith began to prepare for her own death. To family members and friends, she expressed a desire to die peacefully and was terrified of the potential for a lingering or painful death. In preparation for her departure, Edith began a new round of destruction of her personal correspondence in order to protect her privacy.

In 1946, Edith's health had declined to the point that she was no longer able to conduct her correspondence. In September of that year, Edith arranged her will. She had already begun giving away various sums of money and family artifacts to her grandchildren in an effort to prevent them from having to pay an inheritance tax. She left the bulk of her estate, approximately half a million dollars to Archie, Ethel, Eleanor and Belle. That Alice was not included in Edith's will was not intended as a slight, the former First Lady

---

[10] Edward J. Rennehan, Jr., *The Lion's Pride: Theodore Roosevelt and His Family in Peace and War* (New York: Oxford, 1999), p. 240.

[11] Caroli, p. 368-69.

knew that Alice had substantial income from her own sources. Her servants and domestic workers each received monetary awards which ranged from $1,500 to a few hundred dollars. She also directed that Mortlake Manor be held in trust for use by her children and grandchildren.[12]

Throughout 1947 and 1948, Edith remained essentially bedridden. During this period she meticulously planned her funeral. She arranged to be buried in a plot beside Theodore in a simple ceremony in which she even picked the hymns that were sung. In September of 1948, she began to have difficulty breathing. On September 29, she slipped into a coma. At 6:30 the next morning, Edith died at age eighty-seven.

As per her wishes, Edith's funeral was simple and tasteful. Her children ensured that it was carried out in accordance with her wishes. It then fell to Edith and Archie to go through their mother's possessions and effects following her death. Although Edith had been exacting in her will, there remained numerous small items to be divided. Ethel and Archie separated these objects into equal lots and then drew numbers to determine who received each stack.[13]

Following Edith's death in 1948, Ethel worked to turn Sagamore Hill into a historical site. With her own funds and her personal effort, Ethel was able to renovate the family house. In 1953, Sagamore Hill opened to the public as a monument to the matriarch and patriarch of the Oyster Bay Roosevelts, Edith and Theodore.

---

[12] Morris, p. 515.
[13] Caroli, p. 369.

EPILOGUE

Edith Kermit Carow Roosevelt faced the difficult twist of fate by which she outlived not only her husband, but three of her children and all of her close friends. Just a few years prior to her death, Edith was walking in the garden of Sagamore Hill with a secretary she had hired to help her with correspondence and financial accounts. At one point, the young woman observed "Mrs. Roosevelt, you've had such a sad life." Edith responded, "I have no regrets; it's been a full one."[1] This exchange is characteristic of Edith's indomitable personality. Although she faced unbearable emotional hardships during her life she always persevered with quite dignity and remarkable character.

For most of her life, Edith's existence and happiness revolved around her husband. The love story between Edith and Theodore is in itself a timeless expression of true romance. After the death of his first wife, Theodore truly needed Edith in order to recover his sense of self and purpose. For her part, Edith needed Theodore to fulfill herself and to give purpose to her life which otherwise might have emulated that of her sister's. Instead she became the First Lady of both the state of New York and of the United States. She also became the mother of five children and one stepchild and grandmother to a score of grandchildren.

Edith served as the perfect counterbalance to her husband's exuberance. Theodore was headstrong and inclined to forget his station and especially his financial limitations. Edith provided a grounded personality and commonsensical approach to life which kept the family on an even keel. She

---

[1] Quoted in Morris, p. 513.

also furnished the financial management necessary to ensure the fiscal solvency of her clan. Edith's financial acumen allowed the family to maintain its social status even during the periods when Theodore had little real income. She also compensated for Theodore's extravagant spending habits.

Edith's personal inner strength and her enormous self-assurance allowed her to excel in her role as political wife. Edith managed a succession of moves. Usually it was left to her to find a new dwelling, manage the actual logistics of the move and decorate the new home. Edith also had to register the children in school and run the household while her husband often disappeared for lengthy periods hunting or exploring. Edith grew used to this division of labor. Because of her own desire for privacy and personal space, she seemed to grow to enjoy the periods when Theodore and the children left her by herself. The various experiences during her husband's rise prepared Edith for her ultimate political role–that of First Lady.

As First Lady, Edith served as a bridge between the nineteenth and twentieth centuries. She embodied the traditional virtues and egalitarian habits that the American people expected of a presidential spouse in the late 1800s and early 1900s. Her direction of the White House renovation on 1902 was tremendously important in establishing the current division of the mansion into official and private space. She was also responsible for restoring the White House to the center of Washington society through events such as the debuts of Alice and Ethel and Alice's wedding. Her most important contribution as First Lady, however, was the emotional support and comfort that she provided to her husband. While the couple occupied the White House, Edith served as the main check on her husband's actions and behavior. She may not have been his closest political advisor but she was one who had the most success in ensuring that Theodore took care of his physical and emotional health.

Edith also proved to be amazingly adept at public relations. She was the first presidential spouse who truly understood the power and potential of the media. As First Lady, Edith crafted an aura of intimacy and family life in the White House that did not precisely mirror reality. Edith employed a variety of tactics to ensure that she controlled the dissemination of information about the White House. This manipulation of the media was also an indication of the First Lady's strong sense of privacy and her desire to maintain a high degree of privacy even in the most famous house in the United States.

Through the difficult years following her husband's tenure as President, Edith was a pillar of strength for Theodore. She opposed his run for the presidency in 1912, but was instrumental in his recovery from the loss and the assassination attempt. Roosevelt never recovered from Quentin's death during World War I, but Edith continued on and survived the loss of both her son and her husband. As she had done we he married Alice Lee, Edith continued on and developed a new life for herself following the death of her husband. She traveled extensively. She visited Europe, Africa, South America and the Orient and engaged in an around-the-world journey.

These voyages seemed to provide both an escape from the reminders of her former happiness and open the door to a world of adventure that had been suppressed during her marriage. She spent her life on or near the ocean and retained a powerful attachment to the seas until her death. From her youth on the Jersey shores or her experiences at Oyster Bay an in the Caribbean, Edith loved the ocean. She once wrote "All my journeys begin and end with the ocean . . . . I have salt water around my heart."[2]

THE CHILDREN

To Edith one of her most important legacies were her children and she expected each to have "useful" existences. The premature deaths of her husband and sons cast a pall over her the later years of her life. Nonetheless, the former First Lady could take solace in the fact that her other three children lived up to her expectations. Alice, Ethel and Archie all lived long and fruitful lives after Edith's passage. Ethel became known as the "First Lady of Oyster Bay" and led the efforts to preserve the memories of her father and mother. In addition to having Sagamore Hill made a historic monument, Ethel also helped promote the Theodore Roosevelt Association throughout her life. She died in 1977. After leaving the Army in 1945, Archie had considerable success on Wall Street as a founding partner of the brokerage house Roosevelt and Cross. The sad demise of his brother Kermit led Archie to become involved with Alcoholics Anonymous and he was one of the only non-alcoholics to ever serve on the board of the organization. During the Vietnam era he became known for his support of various conservative movements, including the John Birch Society. In 1979, he died at age eighty-five.

Alice outlived all of her siblings. She became a regular Washington fixture known for her political acumen and quick wit. Through the course of her life, she met every President from Benjamin Harrison to Gerald Ford. Following the death of her daughter Paulina, Alice gained custody of her granddaughter Joanna whom she raised. The feisty Alice remained vibrant and full of life until her death at age ninety-six in 1980. At one point, Ethel noted that even though Alice was in her seventies, she "reads the small print in a telephone book without glasses, hears a whisper two blocks away, limber as a cat, deeply interested in all that goes on."[3] Alice survived two mastectomies and practiced yoga into her nineties. As she grew older, Alice ceased being known as "Princess Alice" and came to be referred to as "Washington's *other* monument" although she referred to herself as "Washington's only perambulatory monument."[4]

---

[2] Prindiville, p. 202.

[3] Caroli, p. 431-32.

[4] Carol Felsenthal, *Alice Roosevelt Longworth* (New York: G. P. Putnam's Sons, 1988) p. 260.

BIBLIOGRAPHY

PRIMARY COLLECTIONS

Alice Roosevelt Longworth Papers, Library of Congress, Washington, D.C.
Kermit Roosevelt Papers, Library of Congress, Washington, D.C.
Theodore Roosevelt Collection, Theodore Roosevelt Birthplace National Historic Site, New York City.
Theodore Roosevelt Collection, Widener and Houghton Libraries, Harvard University, Cambridge, Massachusetts.
Theodore Roosevelt Papers, Library of Congress, Washington, D.C.

PUBLISHED WORKS

Brands, H.W. *TR: The Last Romantic*. New York: Basic Books, 1997.
Butt, Archibald W. *Letters*. Lawrence F. Abbot, ed. New York: Doubleday, 1924.
_____. *Taft and Roosevelt*. New York: Doubleday, 1930.
Caroli, Betty Boyd. *First Ladies*. New York: Oxford University Press, 1995.
_____. *The Roosevelt Women*. New York: Basic Books, 1998.
Cheney, Albert Loren. *Personal Memoirs of the Home Life of the Late Theodore Roosevelt*. Washington, D.C.: Cheney Publishing, 1919.
Churchill, Allen. *The Roosevelts: American Aristocrats*. New York: Harper & Row, 1965.
Felsenthal, Carol. *Alice Roosevelt Longworth*. New York: G. P. Putnam's Sons, 1988.

Hagedorn, Hermann. *The Roosevelt Family of Sagamore Hill.* New York: Macmillan, 1954.

Kerr, Joan Paterson. *A Bully Father: Theodore Roosevelt's Letters to His Children.* New York: Random House, 1995.

Leech, Margaret. *In the Days of McKinley.* New York: Harper's, 1959.

Longworth, Alice Roosevelt. *Crowded Hours: Reminiscences of Alice Roosevelt Longworth.* New York, Charles Scribner's Sons, 1933.

Morris, Edmund. *The Rise of Theodore Roosevelt.* New York: Coward, McCann & Geoghegan, 1979.

Morris, Sylvia Jukes. *Edith Kermit Roosevelt: Portrait of a First Lady.* Coward, McCann & Geoghegan, Inc., 1980.

Parsons, Frances. *Perchance Some Day.* Private Publication, 1951

Prindiville, Kathleen. *First Ladies.* New York: MacMillan, 1932.

Pringle, Henry F. *Theodore Roosevelt: A Biography.* New York: Harcourt, Brace & World, 1956.

Putnam, Charleton. *Theodore Roosevelt: The Formative Years, 1858-1886.* Charles Scribner's Sons, 1958.

Rennehan, Edward J., Jr. *The Lion's Pride: Theodore Roosevelt and His Family in Peace and War.* New York: Oxford, 1999.

Robinson, Corrine Roosevelt. *My Brother Theodore Roosevelt.* New York: Charles Scribner's Sons, 1921.

Roosevelt, Kermit. *The Happy Hunting Grounds.* New York: Charles Scribner's Sons, 1921.

Roosevelt, Theodore. *Autobiography.* New York: Macmillan, 1913.

_____. *Diaries of Boyhood and Youth.* New York: Charles Scribner's Sons, 1928.

_____. *Letters.* Vols1-8. Elting E. Morison and John Blum, eds. Cambridge: Harvard University, 1954.

_____. *Theodore Roosevelt's Letters to his Children.* Joseph Bucklin Bishop, ed. New York: Charles Scribner's Sons, 1919.

_____. *Works.* Herman Hagedorn, ed. New York: Charles Scribner's Sons, 1926.

Roosevelt, Theodore Jr. *All in the Family.* New York: Putnam, 1929.

Sferrazza, Carl Anthony. *America's First Families: An Inside View of 200 Years of Private Life in the White House.* New York: Touchstone, 2000.

Teague, Micheal. *Mrs. L: Conversations with Alice Roosevelt Longworth.* Garden City, New York: Doubleday & Company, 1981.

Truman, Margaret. *First Ladies*. New York: Random House, 1996.

Watson, Robert P. "Incorporating the First Lady into the Classroom." *Social Studies* 89/4 (Jul/Aug 1998).

_____. *The President's Wives: Reassessing the Office of First Lady*. Boulder: Lynne Reinner, 2000.

_____. "Ranking the Presidential Spouses." *Social Science Journal* 36/1 (1999): 117-32

Wister, Owen. *Roosevelt: The Story of a Friendship, 1880-1919*. New York: Macmillan. 1930.

ABOUT THE AUTHOR

Tom Lansford is an Assistant Professor of Political Science at the University of Southern Mississippi—Gulf Coast. He has previously published articles in journals such as *Defense Analysis, The Journal of Conflict Resolution, European Security, International Studies,* and *Strategic Studies.* He is the review editor for *The International Journal of Politics and Ethics* and serves on the Governing Board of the National Social Science Association and on the Editorial Board of the journal *White House Studies.* Dr. Lansford is the author of **Evolution and Devolution: The Dynamics of Sovereignty and Security in Post-Cold War Europe** (2000), and coauthor of **Untying the Gordian Knot: Great Power Interests in the Persian Gulf** (1999) and **Teaching Old Dogs New Tricks: International Organizations in the Twenty-First Century** (2000).

INDEX